Gender Equality in Canada

MAINSTREAMING, GOVERNANCE AND BUDGETING

OECD
BETTER POLICIES FOR BETTER LIVES

Please cite this publication as:
OECD (2018), *Gender Equality in Canada: Mainstreaming, Governance and Budgeting*, OECD Publishing, Paris.
http://dx.doi.org/10.1787/9789264301108-en

ISBN 978-92-64-30109-2 (print)
ISBN 978-92-64-30110-8 (PDF)

Photo credits: Cover © Arthimedes/Shutterstock.com

Corrigenda to OECD publications may be found on line at: *www.oecd.org/about/publishing/corrigenda.htm*.

Foreword

There is growing awareness in the global community that gender equality is a cornerstone of inclusive growth. Canada scores well on several metrics of gender equality. Over the past three years, the Canadian government has invested in strengthening the federal governance framework for gender equality by developing institutions, policies, tools and accountability structures to promote gender equality and gender mainstreaming. Canada is now one the few OECD countries where gender analysis is mainstreamed within routine Cabinet policy processes, in accordance with the 2015 *OECD Recommendation on Gender Equality in Public Life* (2015 Recommendation) and the 2013 *OECD Recommendation of the Council on Gender Equality in Education, Employment and Entrepreneurship*.

This OECD Review assesses the policy and institutional framework for delivering gender equality results for Canadians from a whole-of-government perspective, including the systems in place for mainstreaming gender considerations into the policy and decision-making cycles and the budget. It considers the scope for further action with reference to the 2015 Recommendation, and proposes a number of measures to expand gender mainstreaming, strengthen the governance framework for gender equality and advance gender budgeting in Canada. It is designed to assist the Government of Canada in charting a course for achieving better outcomes in gender equality.

The OECD's strong focus on gender equality, in collaboration with other international organisations, has been crucial for raising the profile of the gender agenda internationally. The 2015 Recommendation proposes concrete measures that countries can implement to advance mainstreaming and implementation of gender equality. In this context, the OECD's work on gender budgeting provides insights into how this tool can be best implemented to help deliver gender equality results.

Acknowledgements

This OECD Review is published by the Public Governance Directorate of the OECD under the guidance of Marcos Bonturi, Director for Public Governance, and overall supervision of Jon Blondal, Head of the Budgeting and Public Expenditures Division, and Martin Forst, Head of the Governance Reviews and Partnerships Division.

The Review was overseen by Tatyana Teplova, Senior Counsellor for Gender and Inclusiveness, and Ronnie Downes, Deputy Head of the Budgeting and Public Expenditures Division. It was primarily authored by Pinar Guven (Policy Analyst, Gender Mainstreaming) and Scherie Nicol (Policy Analyst, Gender Budgeting). The authors would like to thank Ronnie Downes and Elena Gentili who made significant contributions. It also benefited from the counsel of Elisabet Borrás Carbajo from the Ministry of Finance and Public Administration in Spain, and peer discussions at the OECD's 2018 Public Governance Committee Meeting.

The authors appreciate the views of experts at the Government of Canada including Justine Akman, Jean Lamirande, Alison McDermott, and Julia Smith. The authors also appreciate the considerable guidance of Michelle d'Auray, Ambassador and Permanent Representative to the OECD, Canada. The authors would like to thank Alba Bosch, Amy Coetzee, Andrew Davies, Gamze Igrioglu and Andrea Uhrhammer from the OECD Secretariat for their contributions. The authors also appreciate the suggestions and recommendations of experts at the OECD from the Economics Department and the Directorate for Employment, Labour and Social Affairs, in particular Monika Queisser, Senior Counsellor and Head of Social Policy Division. Benjamin Jouannes and Lyora Raab provided logistical support, and Bonifacio Agapin, Amelia Godber and Roxana Glavanov provided publication support.

Table of contents

Tables

Figures

Boxes

Abbreviations and acronyms

BI	Behavioural Insights
CAF	Canadian Armed Forces
CEDAW	Convention on the Elimination of all forms of Discrimination Against Women
CoG	Centre of Government
CSO	Civil Society Organisation
EA	Environmental Assessment
GBA	Gender-Based Analysis
GBA+	Gender-Based Analysis Plus
GDP	Gross Domestic Product
GRF	Gender Results Framework
EI	Employment Insurance
FEWO	House of Commons Standing Committee on the Status of Women
FIN	Department of Finance
FINA	House of Commons Standing Committee on Finance
FPT	Federal, Provincial and Territorial
IIU	Impact and Innovation Unit
LGBT	Lesbian, Gay, Bisexual and Transgender
MPs	Members of Parliament
OAG	Office of the Auditor General of Canada
OECD	Organisation for Economic Cooperation and Development
PBO	Parliamentary Budget Office
PCO	Privy Council Office
RDU	Results and Delivery Unit
TBS	Treasury Board Secretariat
SDGs	Sustainable Development Goals
STEM	Science, Technology, Engineering and Mathematics
SWC	Status of Women Canada

Executive summary

Canada has a longstanding commitment to gender equality. Over the past three years, the federal government has developed institutions, policies, tools and accountability structures to promote gender equality and mainstreaming. The appointment of the first Cabinet-level Minister of Status of Women in 2015 was a significant step forward and ensures that gender equality and diversity considerations are brought to the Cabinet table. Another notable development was the creation of the Deputy Ministers' Task Force on Diversity and Inclusion to provide advice on advancing a feminist government. Improvements in the implementation of Gender-Based Analysis Plus (GBA+), which encourages policy designers to undertake a critical analysis of the gender and other diversity-related dimensions of a proposed policy, have also been made in recent years.

Following the 2015 *Report of the Office of the Auditor General on Implementing GBA+* and subsequent recommendations of the House of Commons Standing Committee on the Status of Women, the government made GBA+ mandatory for all Cabinet and Treasury Board submissions. In 2016, GBA+ was integrated into the new Policy on Results, and gender budgeting was introduced by the Department of Finance. In 2017, the Minister of Finance advised departments that all budget proposals should be accompanied by a GBA+ assessment.

In 2018, Canada introduced a government-wide Gender Results Framework to track how the country is performing against key gender equality indicators, proposed to legislate for gender budgeting, created a Centre for Gender, Diversity and Inclusion Statistics to ensure collection of disaggregated data relating to gender and other intersectional factors, and put Status of Women Canada (SWC) on a statutory footing as an official department. These advancements demonstrate Canada's sustained and ambitious commitment to gender equality.

This Review assesses five pillars of governance for gender equality. These pillars are tailored to Canada's specific needs and priorities and build on the provisions of the 2015 OECD Recommendation:

1. The role of a government-wide gender equality strategy
2. Canada's institutional approach to gender equality
3. Policy tools to deliver gender equality results
4. Openness, transparency and accountability in relation to gender equality
5. Advancing gender budgeting in Canada

The OECD Review identifies Canadian strengths in each of these domains. Building on Canada's ambitious gender equality agenda, and to further boost and sustain the effectiveness of ongoing initiatives at the federal level, the Review highlights five key areas where further efforts could underpin improved gender equality results:

First, building on the recently introduced Gender Results Framework, it would be beneficial to develop an over-arching strategy for gender equality to help orient, co-ordinate and drive gender equality initiatives forward, both in the budget process and beyond, as part of Canada's results and delivery agenda. This strategy would provide an opportunity to bring ongoing initiatives by SWC, the Department of Finance (FIN) and the Privy Council Office (PCO) together under the same umbrella.

Second, in the context of formalising SWC as an official department, consideration could be given to scaling up the mandate to expand the focus from solely women and include the focus on broader issues related to gender equality, aligned with the scope of GBA+. This, together with appropriate resourcing, will help enable SWC to become the policy hub and "go-to institution" for issues of gender equality. In parallel, the Deputy Ministers' Task Force on Diversity and Inclusion may wish to reflect on how Canada's institutional landscape might be strengthened to ensure a co-ordinated federal response to gender equality, diversity and inclusion, which are currently being addressed by a number of departments and agencies (e.g. SWC; Department of Canadian Heritage; PCO; Immigration, Refugees and Citizenship Canada).

Third, to maximise the impact of GBA+ on gender equality outcomes, there is room to continue to strengthen its application, scope, quality and rigour, as recognised by the commitment in Budget 2018 to improve the evidence base for GBA+. In doing so, criteria could be established for assessing the quality of GBA+. Such measures could include "results focus", i.e. the extent to which it shows how a proposal will help achieve goals set out in the Gender Results Framework; timeliness, i.e., that the analysis is undertaken early enough to inform policy development; and impact i.e. that the analysis has influenced policy development. The quality of GBA+ can be further improved if there is greater transparency with regard to the GBA+ undertaken across government.

Fourth, accountability for government actions on gender could be strengthened if the Parliament of Canada and the Office of the Auditor General build on their successful interventions in the area of GBA+ by increasing the extent to which a gender perspective is incorporated in their own areas of work. Parliamentary committees should also establish a fixed "home" for scrutiny of gender equality-related content in the budget.

Finally, the Department of Finance can build on the steady progress it has made in gender budgeting efforts by continuing to develop the gender equality-related content presented in the budget and working with stakeholders to have a wide range of gender budgeting tools implemented across the budget cycle. Finance can also ensure that gender budgeting is resilient to political and economic shifts by following through on its proposal to give it legal foundations, continuing to strengthen the corpus of gender budgeting data, ensuring gender budgeting is open to critical perspectives and establishing a framework for measuring its impact.

Summary of recommendations

Recommendation 1: In the context of Canada's stated commitment to gender equality and its results and delivery agenda, the OECD suggests that Canada builds on positive steps it has taken recently by establishing a Gender Results Framework, and use this framework as a foundation for:

- **The development of an overarching gender equality strategy at the federal level, with specific targets, clear allocation of roles, resources and lines of accountability for the whole-of-government, and an accompanying implementation plan and a data strategy**. “Anchoring” and aligning this strategy with the results and delivery agenda of the Government and each department (e.g. mandate letters, Results and Delivery Charters, departmental results frameworks) could maximise its effective implementation. (see Recommendation 9)
- **Engagement with Federal, Provincial and Territorial Governments to work towards a pan-Canadian approach and strategy to gender equality**, and to support Canada in implementing its international commitments such as CEDAW and SDGs. The impact of such an approach could be boosted by aligning policy objectives developed at Federal, Provincial and Territorial (FPT) levels, while respecting the autonomy and flexibility of FPT governments in designing their own policies.

This twin-tracked approach clarifies the overarching gender equality objectives for government as well as civil society and allows Canada to address gender inequalities from a holistic and people-centred perspective. This in turn helps improve policy prioritisation as well as transparency and accountability. There is also the potential for enhanced dialogue between the FPT levels of government, facilitating improved policy coherence and a platform to share good practices.

Recommendation 2: In the context of formalising Status of Women Canada (SWC) as an official department, consideration could be given to scaling up the mandate to expand the focus from solely women and include the focus on broader issues related to gender equality, and align with the broad nature of Gender-based Analysis Plus (GBA+). This, together with the appropriate resourcing, could help SWC to become the government's policy hub and "go-to institution" on issues of gender equality and intersecting identity factors.

Recommendation 3: Canada may wish to reflect on ways to optimise the federal institutional design to allow for a coordinated and coherent response to gender equality, diversity and inclusion. The needs of citizens in these respects are currently being addressed by a number of departments and agencies (e.g., SWC; Department of Canadian Heritage; Privy Council Office (PCO); Immigration, Refugees and Citizenship Canada).The Deputy Ministers' Task Force on Diversity and Inclusion could be an appropriate forum for this reflection.

Recommendation 4: Given Canada's ambitious commitment to improve progress in gender equality, authority and responsibility should be assigned at the Cabinet Committees level to further strengthen the consideration of gender equality and intersectionality issues within Cabinet decision-making.

Recommendation 5: In the context of Canada's new investments to strengthen gender and diversity data, SWC and Statistics Canada - in cooperation with line departments and central agencies - may consider developing a data strategy with an aim to:

- Support the integration of gender indicators in the government's results and delivery approach (see Recommendation 9);
- Remove data related barriers to full implementation of GBA+ and gender-budgeting by the federal departments and agencies; and
- Support the pursuit of progress under the Gender Results Framework and delivery of the proposed gender equality strategy (see Recommendation 1), and anticipate the information needed to track progress against targets in the strategy.

Recommendation 6: To maximise the impact of GBA+ on gender equality outcomes, consideration should be given to establishing criteria for assessing the quality of GBA+ which includes a measure of "results-focus", i.e., the extent to which the GBA+ shows how it will advance progress towards overarching goals set out in the Gender Results Framework, timeliness, i.e., that the analysis is undertaken early enough to inform policy development and impact, i.e., that the analysis has influenced policy development. A stronger role for central agencies and potentially SWC in reviewing GBA+ against these criteria for key submissions to Cabinet could be considered. The quality of GBA+ can be boosted if departmental officials provided with enhanced access to GBA+ undertaken across government for guidance and good practice examples.

Recommendation 7: Given Canada's efforts to further improve the quality and impact of GBA+, priority should be given to supporting departments to integrate GBA+ from the earliest stages of the policy cycle. To help this:

- GBA+ and gender-budgeting should be promoted across the board as organically linked and mutually reinforcing to serve a common goal of improved decision-making and gender outcomes.

- Deeper collaboration between federal departments, SWC and Statistics Canada will ensure that federal departments have sufficient data to develop and monitor gender-sensitive policies (see Recommendation 6).

- Improved use of data at the earlier stages of policy discussions allows more complete GBA+ of policies and helps facilitate evidence-based policy-making.

- Civil society organisations and academic institutions should be recognised as partners who can provide useful information about the impact of government policies. The quality and impact of GBA+ can be boosted if federal departments anchor gender policy development in needs based analysis drawing on consultation with civil society to identify gaps and challenges.

Recommendation 8: Departments should capitalise on existing momentum in relation to gender equality to integrate a "gender+" lens more systematically within all stages of the policy cycle, from design to implementation (including legislative drafting), monitoring and evaluation. The Treasury Board Secretariat (TBS) is already developing guidance for departments in this respect and would be well-placed to also assist departments in its implementation, together with PCO and SWC. To further enable this, on-going reforms should incorporate a gender perspective within departmental planning, sectoral data collection and analysis, and stakeholder engagement. Effective implementation underpins the cultural change required for gender considerations in policy development to go beyond a tick-box exercise.

Recommendation 9: The Gender Results Framework presented as part of Budget 2018 represents an important step forward and provides a useful basis from which gender dimensions can be further integrated into the performance and results framework. Further developments should focus on strengthening the Framework's upstream linkages - to specific gender equality targets set out in a gender equality strategy for Canada – and its downstream linkages to departmental results and delivery frameworks.

Recommendation 10: Recent improvements in government transparency can be further built on by making GBA+ reports available to the public in a manner that is respectful of Cabinet confidences and that does not interfere with the deliberative internal phase of government policy making. The commitment in Budget 2018 to publish GBA+ of all budget items starting in Budget 2019 marks an important step forward in this regard. Analysis should be presented in a way that is clear and easily understood by all stakeholders including SWC, federal departments, Parliament and civil society. The government should consider developing an online repository where gender based analysis can be filed for ease of access.

Recommendation 11: Canada can build on existing good examples of citizen consultation by engaging more systematically with relevant civil society organisations, including gender equality advocacy groups, to seek their views in relation to changes in gender governance and gender policy developments[11]. Civil society perspectives have the potential to enrich the quality and responsive character of gender-responsive, inclusive policy making. Future engagement should benefit from:

- Granting stakeholders opportunities to be informed and consulted in all relevant phases of the policy-cycle. Involvement from the outset ensures stakeholders have genuine opportunities to build and shape gender-sensitive policies;
- Dedicating particular effort to reaching out to the most relevant, vulnerable, underrepresented, or marginalised groups in society, while avoiding the risks of undue influence and policy capture;
- Ensuring clear communication with stakeholders regarding the purpose, scope and process of engagement; and
- Providing feedback to stakeholders on the extent to which the findings of the consultation process have been reflected in subsequent developments.

SWC may also wish to establish an advisory panel of experts from civil society, to help root its actions in local realities and foster trust in society that views and interests of diverse groups are respected.

Recommendation 12: The Parliament of Canada should consider giving the Standing Committee on the Status of Women (FEWO) a strengthened mandate that includes scrutiny of the gender impact of legislative proposals (beyond those directly and explicitly linked to women's issues). A strategic approach where FEWO focuses on legislation that is most significant and relevant would ensure that legislative proposals stand up to challenge for the extent to which they are gender-sensitive. The process would benefit from strong collaboration and coordination between FEWO and committees responsible for reviewing the bill, with FEWO feeding in its assessment in a timely manner (also see Recommendation 13).

Recommendation 13: The Canadian Parliament's successful interventions in the area of GBA+ should be built upon through greater encouragement for parliamentary committees to mainstream gender considerations in their work (for example, through scrutinising the GBA+ assessment associated with legislative proposals they are examining). To undertake this role most effectively, committees would benefit from proactively engaging with relevant civil society organisations, striving for gender balance on witness lists and seeking to engage with underrepresented groups of society.

Recommendation 14: Building on the successful 2009 and 2015 audits, there is scope for the Office of the Auditor General of Canada (OAG) to consider gender considerations in its performance audits, where relevant and practical. This would help the OAG deliver on its commitment to monitoring and supporting the implementation of the SDGs, including Goal 5 relating to Gender Equality.

Recommendation 15: The Department of Finance (FIN) can build on progress made in gendering the 2017 and 2018 budgets, through continuing to provide comprehensive gender equality-related content in budget, serving as a robust accountability tool to further gender equality. It can be strengthened through:

- Delivering on the commitment to provide information on how all main budget measures, including cuts, are anticipated to impact gender equality.
- Increased recognition, where possible, of intersectionality and how key budget measures might impact different groups of society, such as Indigenous women, women with disabilities, and different gender identities.
- Presenting analysis showing how individual and aggregate tax and benefit measures in the budget are anticipated to affect different groups of women and men, how the budget impacts incentives for second earners to enter formal employment and the ability of different groups of men and women to access public services.
- Developing capacity for budget tagging to highlight and monitor the total money disbursed through the budget in order to achieve gender equality goals.

Recommendation 16: FIN can work with government stakeholders to mobilise, coordinate and strengthen the wide range of gender budgeting tools being implemented across the budget cycle in Canada. A comprehensive approach to gender budgeting should include a rolling programme of gender budget baseline analysis and further incorporation of a gender perspective in *ex post* gender budgeting tools such as evaluations and spending review.

Recommendation 17: To facilitate parliamentary scrutiny of gender budgeting - opening the way for substantive engagement on policy priorities and progress - a fixed "home" for scrutiny of gender equality-related content in the budget should be established at parliament. The engagement of the FEWO Committee in scrutiny of the impact of Budget 2018 on women and girls is a positive step forward. In the longer term, a more robust accountability model may involve both the Finance and FEWO Committees holding a joint session to conduct scrutiny of gender equality-related content in the budget. Committee(s) would be expected to engage with the Finance Minister and the Minister for Status of Women, as well as gender equality advocacy groups, in undertaking this scrutiny.

Recommendation 18: The PBO's independent authority and expertise would lend itself well to independent assessment of equality-related content in the budget. If the PBO is to engage in this area, a useful starting point could be the provision of independent distributional analysis on the extent to which gender equality is promoted through the tax and benefit policies in the budget proposal. Input in this respect has the potential to improve budget transparency and support broader parliamentary scrutiny of the budget.

Recommendation 19: FIN should continue to work with government stakeholders to build an effective and sustainable approach to gender budgeting, which is resilient to political and economic shifts, through:

- Providing legal foundations for gender budgeting;
- Acting as an advocate for gender budgeting;
- Building a corpus of gender-disaggregated data;
- Ensuring gender budgeting is open to critical perspectives; and
- Measuring the impact of gender budgeting.

Recommendation 20: **FIN and SWC could facilitate a coordinated approach to gender budgeting across different levels of government through convening a pan-Canadian working group on gender budgeting**. This would aim to share best practice, and exchange insights on how policy goals might best be coordinated and sequenced among the Canadian community of policy makers.

Notes

[1] See the 2017 OECD Recommendation of the Council on Open Government.

Chapter 1. Gender equality in Canada: the state of play

This chapter outlines Canada's relative position in the OECD for key international gender indicators and provides a historical context on government action in relation to gender equality. The chapter also outlines the current political commitment to a 'feminist agenda' in Canada, and looks at the extent to which this has acted as a catalyst for the federal administration to accelerate the implementation of gender equality initiatives. Finally, the chapter outlines the role of government-wide gender equality policy strategies at federal and sub-national levels in Canada, building on the recently launched Gender Results Framework.

1.1. Introduction

Canada has a tradition of support for gender equality, a principle which is enshrined at the constitutional level and which has been advanced through political and administrative initiatives over successive governments. This has contributed to Canada scoring well in international metrics of gender equality, particularly in the area of educational attainment and women's participation in the labour market. But challenges remain, for example in the gender wage gap; in women's under-representation in engineering and computer sciences education subjects; women's access to leadership positions in the private sector; and gender-based violence. Canada's Indigenous peoples face additional challenges in society and in public life, and this can compound the gender inequalities they experience. This chapter outlines Canada's relative position in the OECD for key international gender indicators and provides a historical context on government action in relation to gender equality. The chapter also outlines the current political commitment to a 'feminist agenda', and looks at the extent to which this has acted as a catalyst for the federal administration to accelerate the implementation of gender equality initiatives.

1.2. Gender equality: policy achievements, impacts and challenges

1.2.1. Gender equality in leadership

In the political sphere, in 2015, the federal Government appointed Canada's first-ever gender parity Cabinet in which key ministerial positions such as Justice and Foreign Affairs are held by women. This delivered a clear signal, both nationally and internationally, about the high-level commitment to gender equality and inclusion as central principles of public governance.

Despite these gains in equal representation in the Cabinet, women remain underrepresented in the Canadian Parliament. Only 26% of Canada's Members of Parliament (MPs) in the House of Commons are women, compared to the OECD average of 29% in 2017 (see Figure 1.1). In the Senate, the representation of women is somewhat higher: 43% of Senators are women, a significant increase from 36% in 2011. At the sub-national level, women currently represent 29.6% (222 out of 751) of all provincial and territorial legislators across Canada (OECD, 2017[1])[1].

Figure 1.1. Share of women parliamentarians and legislated gender quotas, 2015 and 2017

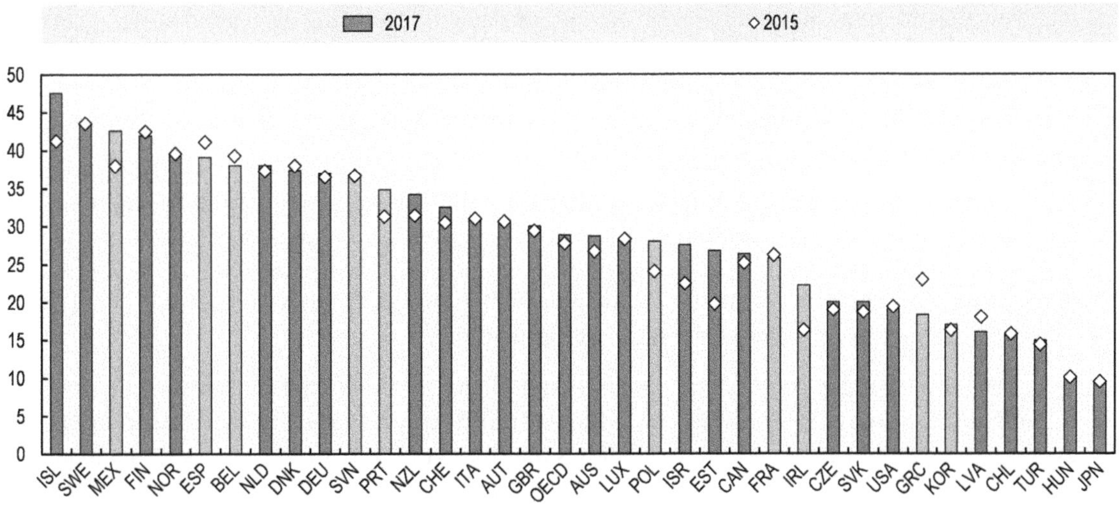

Note: Bars in light blue represent countries with lower or single house parliaments with legislated candidate quotas as of as of March 2017. Data refer to the share of women parliamentarians recorded as of 1 January 2017 and 1 December 2015.
Source: Inter-Parliamentary Union (IPU) PARLINE (database), and IDEA Quota Project (database).

In the private sector, while there has been an upward trend in the representation of women in senior management and on corporate boards in Canada, there is room for progress. Women in director positions continue to account for a minority of Canadian board seats. In 2016, the share of seats held by women on boards of directors in publicly listed companies was 19.4% (comparable to an OECD average of 20% OECD)[2].

1.2.2. Gender equality in the labour market

Canada has one of the smallest gender employment gaps in the OECD but despite recent progress in this area, gender gaps remain. This remains a high priority for the government because figures show that advancing women's equality in Canada has the potential to add $150 billion in incremental GDP in 2026 (or a 0.6% increase to annual GDP growth) (McKinsey Global Institute, 2017[2]). Employment rates for immigrant women are also higher than the OECD average and relatively close to women born in Canada (OECD, 2017[5]). However, the employment rate gap is particularly large between recent immigrant women (i.e. those in Canada for 5 years or less) and women born in Canada (58.5% for recent immigrant women aged 25-54 versus 82% for native-born women aged 25-54). The Government of Canada implements an overarching strategy, the Employment Equity Act, to improve gender equality in Canadian civil service employment. The government has also established hiring targets for women and men, based on the availability of women and men in the specific professional areas in the labour market. As of March 2016, women comprised 54.4% of the Federal public service workforce, while the Workforce Availability for Women was estimated at 52.5%.

Low employment rates are concentrated among women with young children, including single mothers (OECD (forthcoming), 2018[3]). (Moyser, 2017[4]) found that the gender employment gap is greater in localities with high childcare fees than in those with lower childcare costs in Canada. While family cash benefits – notably, the Canada Child Benefit - provide a source of funds for families to pay for childcare, they do not reduce the marginal cost of childcare (OECD (forthcoming), 2018[3]). Additionally, research shows that there can be a high penalty for flexibility in some high-wage occupations, showing that rewards to working long hours are an obstacle for closing the gender pay gap (Goldin, 2014[5]). Over time, the underrepresentation of women in top jobs accounts for a growing share of the gender gap, after taking into consideration the usual list of factors including education, occupation, industry, etc. (Canadian Institute for Advanced Research & Vancouver School of Economics, 2016[6])

Men's take-up of parental leave in Canada is low with the exception of the province of Québec. Fathers often earn more than their partners, and it usually makes economic sense for the mother to take the bulk of the paid leave. In 2017, Canada introduced an option to extend the duration of Employment Insurance (EI) parental leave benefits from 12 months to 18 months at a lower income replacement rate.

The gender wage gap in Canada persists and there is significant progress required. Examining the hourly rate, a measure which partially controls for the fact that men on average work more hours than women, shows that for every dollar of hourly wages a man working full-time earns in Canada, the average Canadian full-time female employee earns around 88 cents – placing Canada 15th out of 29 OECD countries based on the hourly gender wage gap (Government of Canada, 2018[7]). As one means to help overcome this, the Government of Canada has committed to introduce pay equity legislation in 2018 to ensure that employees in federally regulated workplaces (Government of Canada, 2018[7]). Although a direct impact of this legislation on the wage gap is not anticipated.

Figure 1.2. Share of women in Senior Management positions in Central Government

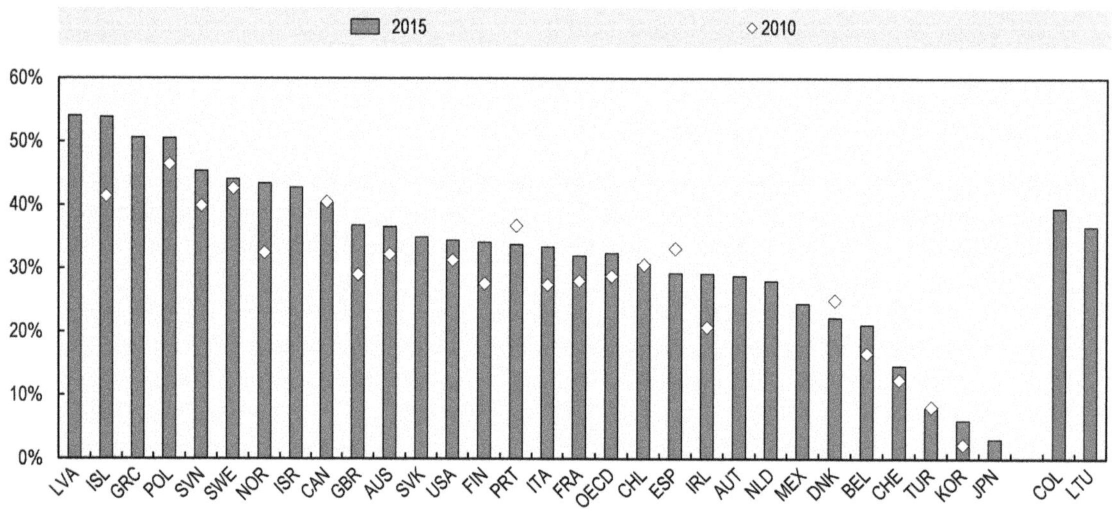

Note: OECD average excludes Austria, Latvia, Greece, Israel, Japan, Mexico, the Netherlands and the Slovak Republic due to missing time series.
Source: OECD (2016) Survey on the Composition of the workforce in Central/federal Governments.

Figure 1.3. Gender pay gap across OECD and G20 countries

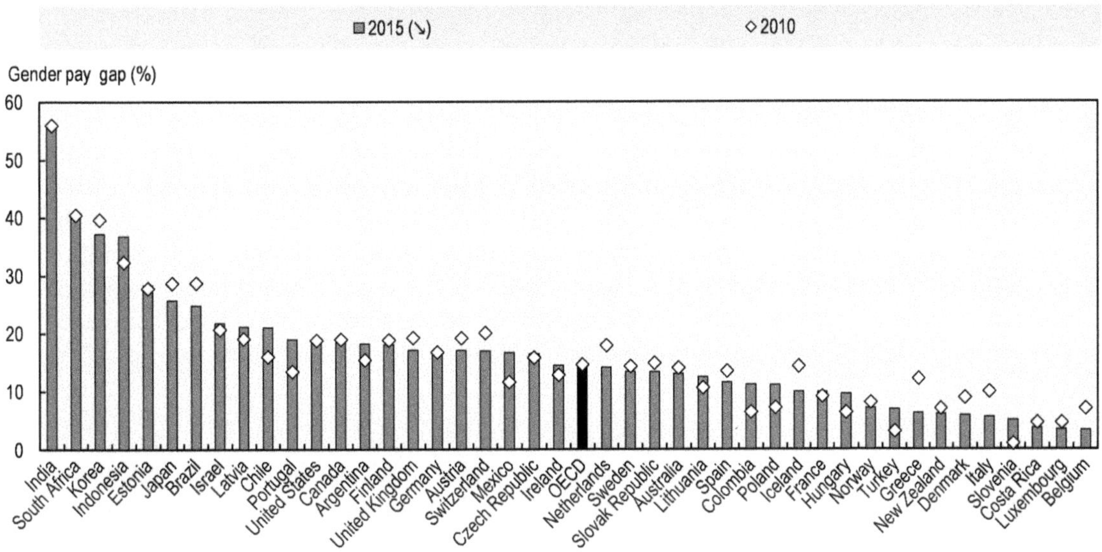

Note: The gender gap in median monthly earnings is defined as the difference between male and female median monthly earnings divided by male median monthly earnings, for full-time employees. Full-time employees are those individuals with usual weekly working hours equal to or greater than 30 hours per week.

a) Data refer to weekly earnings for Australia, Canada, India, Ireland, the United Kingdom and the United States, and to hourly wages for Denmark, Greece, Iceland, New Zealand, Portugal and Spain.

b) Data refer to 2014, not 2015, for Argentina, Belgium, Brazil, Estonia, France, Germany, Indonesia, Italy, Latvia, Lithuania, Luxembourg, the Netherlands, New Zealand, Poland, Slovenia, Spain, Switzerland and Turkey. They refer to 2013 for Sweden, 2012 for India and South Africa, and 2011 for Israel. Data refer to 2011, not 2010, for Brazil, Chile and Costa Rica.

Source: (OECD, 2017[1])

1.2.3. Women in education

In the education sphere, while women earn more bachelor's degrees than men in Canada (60%), there are important and persistent gender differences in the subjects that young men and women study at college and university. There are lower proportions of Canadian women in STEM fields and in doctoral studies (OECD, 2017[1]), where Canadian men represent 67% of all STEM graduates (Government of Canada, 2018[8]). Conversely, Canadian women are disproportionately represented in the studies of health and education, accounting for about 80% of all graduates in Personal and Social Education (PSE). Moreover, OECD research shows that Canadian girls and women perform worse than their male peers in mathematics as teenagers (OECD, 2017[1]) and further research suggests that barriers to closing this STEM education gender gap are related to implicit bias and gender stereotypes, as well as to broader socio-economic, structural and cultural factors (Wells, 2018[9]). It appears that these gaps become greater as they move into adulthood; Canadian women also have lower scores in financial literacy (OECD, 2017[1]). These gender gaps in academic fields are reflected in the labour force and while women have made headway into certain male-dominated industries and occupations (those with 25% or less women in total employment), there is still a significant gender gap in many occupations. Women continue to be highly overrepresented in clerical, service, and health-related occupations in Canada, while men tend to be over overrepresented in craft, operator, and labourer jobs (Catalyst, 2017[10]). Male-dominated industries are especially vulnerable to masculine stereotypes which make it difficult for women to progress and excel, and male-dominated occupations generally pay more than female-dominated ones (Catalyst, 2017[10]), further entrenching the gender pay gap.

1.2.4. Gender-based violence

There is room for progress regarding tackling gender-based violence. According to Statistics Canada findings, women self-reported slightly more than 1.2 million violent victimisation incidents, representing 56% of all violent incidents, and women have a 20% higher risk of being victimised than men (Mahony, 2011[11]). SWC indicates that the economic costs of intimate partner violence against Canadian women is $4.8 billion annually and the economic costs of sexual assault/other sexual offences against Canadian women are estimated to be $3.6 billion annually. To tackle this, in 2017, SWC developed Canada's first federal Strategy to Prevent and Address Gender-Based Violence.

1.2.5. Indigenous women

Indigenous women and girls are particularly vulnerable to gender inequalities in Canada. Indigenous women are over three times more likely than non-Indigenous women to report spousal violence. In fact, being Indigenous is a key risk factor on its own for experiencing violence (Status of Women Canada, 2017[12]). Work by the FEWO Committee has also highlighted a crisis of missing and murdered Indigenous women and girls in Canada. The current government has put this crisis at the heart of its agenda through the Speech of the Throne, which lays out Government's top priorities, and launched an inquiry into missing and murdered Indigenous women and girls. Indigenous women also face particular challenges in educational attainment and labour market outcomes and access to justice. With regard to the gender wage gap, Indigenous women employed full-time earn 26 percent less than non-Indigenous men, and Indigenous women with a university degree earn 33 percent less (McInturff and Lambert, 2016[13]).

1.3. Government action in relation to gender equality: a historical context

Canada has undertaken a series of initiatives over the past half-century to promote gender equality. Key milestones over this period are set out in Box 1.1. Canada has also championed, among other countries, the development and adoption of the *2015 OECD Recommendation of the Council on Gender Equality in Public Life* (the 2015 Recommendation). In the past two decades, the Canadian approach to GBA+ has evolved into a modern, sophisticated and distinctive tool across the OECD for the mainstreaming of gender equality in public policy making (see Chapter 2).

Box 1.1. Milestones in relation to the Canadian Government's commitment to gender equality

Key milestones in gender equality can be categorised into three periods: Making Commitments (1970 - 1995), Setting the Stage (1995 - 2002) and Building Accountability (2003 - present):

Making Commitments (1970 - 1995)

- 1970: Report of the Royal Commission on the Status of Women investigated all matters pertaining to the status of women in Canada and was presented to the Parliament.
- 1971: The position of Minister responsible for the Status of Women was created.
- 1981: Canada ratified the Convention on the Elimination of All Forms of Discrimination against Women (CEDAW).
- 1982: The Canadian Charter of Rights and Freedoms guaranteeing equality rights was enacted.
- 1985: The Canadian Human Rights Act prohibiting gender-based discrimination was adopted.

Setting the Stage (1995 - 2002)

- 1995: Canada adopted the Beijing Declaration and the Platform for Action.
- 1995: The Government of Canada committed to conducting GBA on all future legislation, policies, and programmes and developed the Federal Plan for Gender Equality (1995-2000).
- 2000: The Agenda for Gender Equality, a five year government-wide strategy to accelerate the implementation of GBA, was adopted.

Building Accountability (2003 - present)

- 2004: The Standing Committee on the Status of Women (FEWO) was established in the House of Commons.
- 2009: The Office of the Auditor General published an audit of Gender-Based Analysis.
- 2009: Status of Women Canada and the central agencies developed a Departmental Action Plan on Gender-Based Analysis.
- 2011: Status of Women Canada rebranded GBA as GBA+ to factor in diverse identity circumstances into the analysis.
- 2015: The first-ever full Minister for the Status of Women was appointed.
- 2015: The Auditor General published an audit on Implementing Gender-Based Analysis.
- 2016: The application of GBA+ is made mandatory for all Memorandums to Cabinet and Treasury Board submissions.
- 2016: Status of Women Canada, the Privy Council Office and the Treasury Board Secretariat release the GBA+ Action Plan (2016-2020).
- 2017: Federal Budget 2017 was accompanied by a Gender Budgeting Statement for the first time.

Source: (Status of Women Canada,(n.d.)[14])

1.4. The arrival of a "feminist government" in 2015

In 2015, the newly elected Government signalled its wish to advance its commitment to feminism and feminist government in both domestic and foreign policy spheres[2]. Arising from this heightened focus on gender equality, diversity and inclusion, the systems and processes of policy making have been re-assessed and adapted with a view of enhancing their impact[3]. In the domestic sphere, the public commitment has been directly reflected within the mandates of all ministers who are expected to ensure diversity and gender parity in leadership positions. The federal Government took steps to boost the role and prominence of the federal gender apparatus[4]. Canada also released its first-ever Gender Statement as an integral part of the federal budget in 2017 and further advanced gender budgeting in 2018 (see Chapter 5). In the foreign policy sphere, the Government rolled out its first Feminist International Assistance Policy and it has put gender equality as one of the key priorities for Canada's G7 Presidency in 2018.

Securing leadership and commitment to gender equality at the highest political level is a vital ingredient for advancing gender equality, as stressed in the 2015 Recommendation. While it is soon to evaluate the impact of this commitment in the long run, in the short term, the OECD noted that the federal administration has been incentivised to demonstrate better results for gender equality. The high level political commitment has also increased the attention given to gender-based analysis across Departments. While independent civil society organisations and women's associations recognise that there remains important room for progress in several policy spheres, most such organisations recognise current efforts as crucial steps towards a supportive, enabling environment for gender equality policy.

The following section provides an overview of gender equality gains in recent years.

1.4.1. A government reflective of gender equality and diversity

The 2015 Recommendation promotes correcting gender inequalities through a coordinated, coherent approach to gender equality across all areas of public policy making, including in senior management and political representation. The Government of Canada has moved to correct gender imbalances in leadership appointments in the public sector. An example is the creation of Canada's first gender-balanced Cabinet, together with the appointment of women to key ministerial portfolios such as Foreign Affairs, Justice and Labour. This has resulted in an increase of female ministers from 30.8% to 50% in Canada, well above the OECD average of 28% in 2017. Canada now ranks among the top countries across the OECD in terms of women in ministerial positions at the federal/national level[5] (see Figure 1.4).The Prime Minister has also mandated all Ministers to ensure diversity and gender parity in leadership positions within their portfolios.

Figure 1.4. Share of women ministers, 2015 and 2017

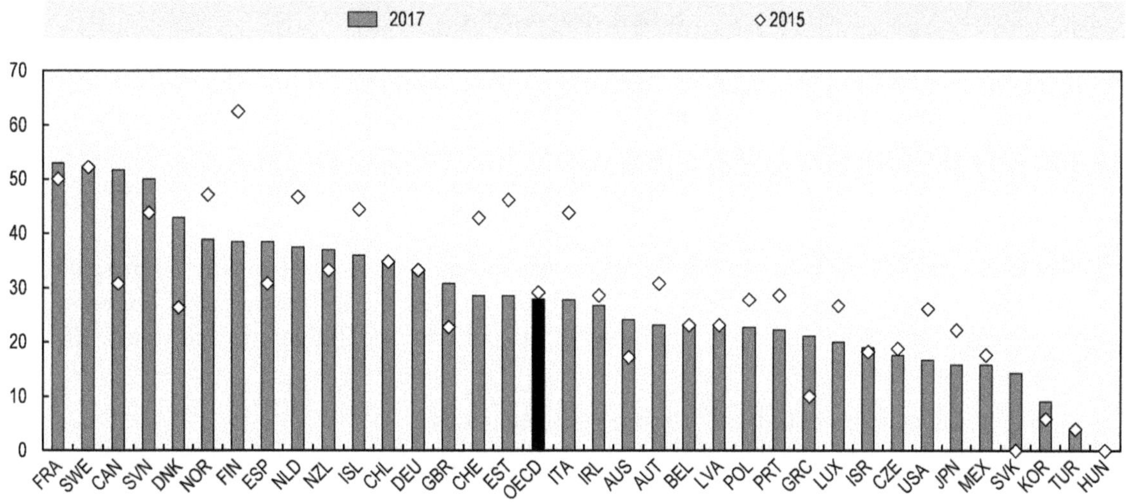

Note: Data for Iceland for 2017 is provided by the Government of Iceland.
Source: Inter-Parliamentary Union (IPU) and UN Women "Women in Politics", 2015 and 2017.

These high level political developments have put positive pressure across the federal administration to demonstrate better results on gender equality. An example comes from the Canadian Armed Forces (CAF) where the Chief of the Defence Staff set a target to increase the percentage of female staff from 15% to at least 25% by 2026 (see Box 1.2).

In this example, the use of behavioural insights (BI) was instrumental in developing a more gender balanced approach to recruitment. The use of BI has gained traction in many OECD countries to help institutions better design, implement, and enhance interventions across a range of topics (OECD, 2017[15]). In the area of gender equality, a growing body of evidence shows that BI can be helpful in reducing conscious and unconscious gender bias and stereotypes in governments, boardrooms and classrooms (Bohnet, 2016[16]). Given the high potential, the Impact and Innovation Unit could consider the application of BI in relation to gender equality and diversity a routine element of its portfolio. The Unit would also benefit from applying a gender lens, where possible, to the support that it provides to departments.

Box 1.2. Increasing the recruitment of women into the Canadian Armed Forces using behavioural insights

In November 2015, the Canadian Armed Forces (CAF) approached the Impact and Innovation Unit (IIU) – a unit in the PCO which experiments with new applying approaches to solve complex policy and programme challenges - for help with increasing the number of women staff. The Chief of the Defence Staff set a target to increase the percentage from the current 15% to at least 25% by 2026.

A research project was designed by the IIU to support this goal using behavioural insights (BI).The research looked at how BI could be applied to the recruitment process; recruitment marketing and communications and policies and guidelines and made 20 recommendations including:

- Using gender-neutral job titles for all occupations;
- Mandating gender disclosure on job application forms and including a third gender option;
- Running randomised controlled trials to test different types of applicant correspondence and identifying the most effective message format;
- Researching possible barriers in five key CAF policy areas: deployments and relocation; leave without pay; childcare support; long-term commitment/ability to resign; and culture/diversity.

Although this project focused on female recruitment, many of the findings apply to all CAF applicants, regardless of gender, and the recommendations have the potential to enhance the overall ease, effectiveness and success of the CAF's recruitment process.

Source: (Government of Canada, 2016[17])

1.5. Sustaining the momentum on gender equality

The Government of Canada has invested in strengthening the federal gender apparatus at an unprecedented pace. For the purposes of this report, the federal gender apparatus can be described as institutions, policies, tools and accountability structures to promote gender equality and mainstreaming at the federal level.

From a historical perspective, the development of the gender equality apparatus at the federal level has not been linear. As in number of OECD countries, the gender apparatus in Canada has experienced rollbacks contingent on the shifts in power. For example, Status of Women Canada (SWC), which is the main federal government organisation mandated to coordinate policy with respect to women's rights, has seen its mandate narrowed and budget significantly reduced throughout different administrations. A number of regional offices were also closed down. The absence of a legislative underpinning for SWC has reinforced the organisation's vulnerability to the shifts in power (see Chapter 2).

The implementation of the Cabinet commitment to GBA+ has also been uneven across federal departments. Almost 15 years after the Cabinet commitment to GBA, the Office of the Auditor General (OAG) reported in 2009 that there was no evidence of the analysis being considered or documented in decision-making. A follow-up audit by the OAG in 2015 concluded that while SWC made progress in supporting the departmental implementation of gender-based analysis, analysis by departments was still missing, incomplete or inconsistent (see Chapter 3).

Recent developments go some way to address these challenges. The appointment of the first Cabinet-level Minister of Status of Women in November 2015 marks a step forward in terms of strengthening the federal gender apparatus, and ensures that gender equality and diversity considerations are systematically brought to the Cabinet table. In 2018, to further solidify and formalise the important role of SWC and its Minister – and in accordance with preliminary OECD recommendations in the preparation of this Report - the Federal Budget announced the introduction of departmental legislation to make SWC an official Department of the Government of Canada, almost fifty years after its establishment. The funding of SWC was also significantly restored and increased between 2015 and 2018. There is scope to further build on these advances to sustain them into the future, as discussed under Chapter 2.

A further development in Budget 2018 which aligned with preliminary OECD recommendations was the introduction of a Gender Results Framework (GRF) which establishes a whole-of-government tool to track how Canada is performing against key indicators relating to gender equality.

Another important development has been the creation of the Deputy Ministers' Task Force on Diversity and Inclusion (the Task Force) co-chaired by the Deputy Ministers of SWC and Immigration, Refugees and Citizenship Canada. The mandate of the Task Force is to examine and formulate advice on how to promote inclusion and implement the Government's commitment to a feminist domestic agenda. Its recommendations are due to be formulated by summer 2018. In the absence of an overarching federal government strategy in relation to gender equality, the recommendations of the Task Force will be instrumental in guiding future gender equality reforms, whose progress can be tracked using the recently introduced GRF.

Improvements in the implementation of gender-based analysis plus (GBA+) have also been implemented in recent years. Following the 2015 OAG audit of GBA+ and the subsequent recommendations of the House of Commons Standing Committee on the Status of Women (FEWO), the government made mandatory since 2016 that evidence be provided to demonstrate that GBA+ has been considered and completed as necessary for all submissions brought before Cabinet and the Treasury Board (see Chapter 3). In the same year, GBA+ was integrated into the government's new Policy on Results (also see Chapter 3). In 2017, the Minister of Finance advised departments that all budget proposals should also be accompanied by a GBA+ assessment (see Chapter 5). Canada is now one the few OECD countries where gender analysis is mainstreamed within routine Cabinet policy process, in accordance with the 2015 Recommendation. Work is currently underway to make GBA+ mandatory for regulatory impact analysis. Early indications show that these initiatives have already yielded positive impacts on the GBA+ capacity within federal departments and agencies. In addition, since GBA+ became mandatory, more departments appear to be collecting gender-disaggregated data (Status of Women Canada, 2018). Looking ahead, there is scope to further embed GBA+ across the different phases of the policy cycle, from problem definition to evaluation and impact analysis. Chapter 3 examines in more detail how the achievements from this wave of reforms can be consolidated and built upon.

Important advances have also been made regarding accountability and monitoring structures for GBA+. These include giving the Privy Council Office (PCO) and the Treasury Board Secretariat (TBS) a stronger "challenge" function in relation to GBA+; introducing an annual GBA+ implementation Survey sent to Deputy Ministers by SWC; and a commitment to report to the House of Commons Public Accounts Committee on the implementation of GBA+.

Other strides in advancing the federal gender apparatus on the policy side include the launch of a National Inquiry into Missing and Murdered Indigenous Women and Girls in 2016 as well as the adoption of Canada's first Strategy to Prevent and Address Gender-Based Violence in 2017. These developments address historical gaps in the federal governance processes for gender equality.

1.5.1. The role of gender equality strategies at federal and sub-national levels

Canada has a unique opportunity to reverse persistent gaps in gender equality. The establishment of a Gender Results Framework as part of Budget 2018 provides strong foundations upon which a commonly agreed upon strategy for gender equality and diversity can be built, in line with the 2015 Recommendation, to boost progress in Canada. Such a strategy would provide a policy umbrella under which gender mainstreaming and targeted initiatives meet to advance society-wide goals for gender equality. Indeed, the development of a gender equality strategy has become common practice across the OECD. Currently more than half of all OECD countries have national or federal multi-year gender equality strategies in place, although their implementation and effectiveness varies across countries (see e.g. Box 1.3).

Specifics in relation to a federal gender equality strategy

Development of a federal gender equality strategy would not be a new exercise for Canada. SWC published Canada's first Federal Plan for Gender Equality in 1995 in collaboration with 24 federal departments and agencies in response to the United Nations' call for member states to formulate a national plan to advance the situation of women. In 2000, SWC developed the second five year government-wide strategy to accelerate the implementation of GBA. These experiences have provided valuable lessons for future strategies. In particular, it has become clear that these strategies are most effective when there is buy-in from central agencies and line departments; identification of adequate resources; focus on achieving outcome oriented objectives; and the identification of clear lines of accountability at the highest political level.

A number of initiatives are underway at the federal level provide useful ground work for the development of an overarching gender equality strategy. This includes the recent investment in a new centre for Gender Diversity and Inclusion Statistics; the preparation of Diversity and Inclusion Charter led by the PCO; and the Gender Results Framework (GRF) introduced as part of Budget 2018 which lays out government's priorities for gender equality. The development of the GRF marked an important step towards strengthening transparency of and accountability for gender equality priorities in Canada.

A similar exercise by the Victorian Government in Australia has shown early indications of success. In 2015, the state government committed to achieving gender parity across all paid government board positions, with women's representation standing at just 38% at the time. The following year the government launched its gender equality strategy, incorporating this goal as one of its priorities. The annual progress report for the strategy recorded progress against strategic priorities. The Victorian Government's gender equality strategy and related annual progress reports assisted transparency and accountability and helped the government make progress in relation to its gender equality commitments. As of 2018, 53% of paid public board positions were held by women (The Victorian Government, 2018[18]).

While the Canadian GRF is intended to become a whole-of-government tool to track gender equality results, the current commitment is to apply it to Budget 2018 and future budgets. There is scope to strengthen interlinkages with the on-going initiatives of SWC and PCO, and complement it with an implementation plan – in the context of the government's results and delivery agenda - so that there is further clarity among government and civil society stakeholders about:

- Which institutional actors are accountable for progress in relation to different objectives in the GRF;
- How the government's gender equality priorities are linked to the results and delivery frameworks of each department (see Chapter 3); and
- How the government can maximise the impact of its gender mainstreaming tools (e.g., GBA+ in policies, budgets, regulations, procurement, etc.) to achieve the objectives in the GRF.

In rolling out an implementation strategy for the GRF, the government's *Action Plan for Gender-Based Analysis Plus (GBA+) for 2016-2020* puts forward a comprehensive and sophisticated governance plan to implement GBA+ and can provide a useful foundation. Moving forward, there are opportunities to strengthen understanding and knowledge on gender gaps across federal departments and their policy areas, highlighted by federal departments as a common barrier to full implementation of GBA+. There are also opportunities to clarify the gender outcomes that are being sought through the use of GBA+ and gender budgeting (although some individual departments have taken notable steps in this area in recent years).

There are promising examples of gender equality implementation strategies across the OECD that Canada may draw inspiration from. Further details on the content and governance processes for each of these strategies are presented in Box 1.3. All of these strategies adopt a 'dual approach' whereby targeted initiatives are coupled with gender mainstreaming requirements in line with the 2015 Recommendation.

Box 1.3. Examples of gender equality strategies across the OECD

Finland

In May 2016, Finland launched its *Government Action Plan for Gender Equality 2016 – 2019*, consisting of an overarching gender equality strategy of around thirty measures covering all ministries. The strategy contributes to meeting international commitments laid out in the United Nation's Convention on the Elimination of All Forms of Discrimination against Women and the European Council's Istanbul Convention, as well as the government's programme for the promotion of equality between women and men.

The Action Plan was built on the directions given by experts and key stakeholders consulted during the preparation process and it was later finalised in collaboration with the ministries. It offers concrete actions and realistic goals articulated around six areas: labour market equality, reconciliation of work, family and parenthood, gender equality in education and sports, intimate partner violence and violence against women, men's wellbeing and health and decision-making that promotes gender equality. For each of these areas, the strategy sets objectives to be achieved during the government's term and others for the long-term. Besides the specific thematic measures that fall into its respective ministry, the plan also includes measures to ensure that all ministries assess the gender impacts of their activities and take them into account in their decision-making.

The Ministry of Social Affairs and Health is responsible for the coordination of the work related to the Action Plan. However, the Action Plan requires extensive inter-ministerial cooperation and commitment. A working group has been appointed to support and monitor the implementation of the plan and report to government.

Spain

In 2014, the Spanish Government launched the government's *Strategic Plan for Equal Opportunities 2014-2016.* The strategy was developed with the aim of ensuring a high degree of consensus and viability. To this end, the plan drew on work by the Spanish Women's Institute and existing European strategies such as the EU's *Strategy for Equality between Women and Men 2010-2015* and *Europe 2020 Strategy*, as well as reports and proposals from the Equality Commissions of both the Spanish Congress and Senate. Objectives and measures were set in collaboration with line ministries. The Plan was also sent to the Council for Women's Participation for final consultation.

The *Strategic Plan for Equal Opportunities 2014-2016* is articulated around seven action axes: labour market and gender pay gap equality, balance between personal, family, and work life and co-responsibility in family responsibilities, eradication of violence against women, women's participation in political life and economical and social spheres, education, development of gender equality actions in sectorial politics and mainstreaming gender in the Government's policies and actions.

In each of the seven axes, the strategy provides an overview of the situation and sets specific objectives, lines of action and planned measures. For some axes, special measures targeting rural and especially vulnerable women were introduced.

The plan includes a clear governance scheme, based on a classification of three disparate types of agents:

- Responsible Agents: Each of the Ministerial departments and in particular the Ministry for Health, Social Affairs and Equality are responsible for the implementation of the plan in its competency areas.
- Support Agents: Equality Units of the Ministries are responsible for facilitating and ensuring line ministries execute the plan's measures.
- Coordination Agents: The General Authority for Equal Opportunities and the Women's

Institute are responsible for the preparation, monitoring and evaluation of the Plan, as well as coordinating the Equality Units and general plan coordination.

The Plan also commits to developing an Evaluation Program which would include a selection of indicators corresponding to the Plan's objectives, to allow for better monitoring, assess the level of implementation and evaluate the final results.

Australia, Government of Victoria

In 2016, the State Government of Victoria launched *Safe and Strong: A Victorian Gender Equality Strategy*, which sets out founding reforms that lay the groundwork and set a new standard for action by the Victorian Government on reducing violence against women and delivering gender equality. *Safe and Strong* has been informed by the diverse voices and experiences of more than 1,200 Victorians through consultations with specific groups and communities across a wide range of sectors and industries, including Indigenous Victorians, people with a disability, seniors, young people, culturally diverse communities and LGBTI Victorians. The Strategy provides a needs analysis and draws on global evidence of what works in gender equality. The Strategy lays out long-term outcomes that the Victorian Government aspires to reach and its commitment to measure and track progress through an outcomes framework.

Sources: (Government of Finland, 2016[19]); (Government of Spain, 2014[20]); (The Victorian Government, 2018[18])

Specifics in relation to a pan-Canadian gender equality strategy

Canada has a broad range of longstanding international gender-related commitments, including CEDAW, the SDGs, the Beijing Platform for Action and OECD Gender Recommendations. There is scope to complement these external commitments with an over-arching Canada-specific strategy based on the gender equality and inclusion priorities that are most relevant, and that can feed most directly into federal policy making. Indeed, in the concluding observations of the latest periodic reports of Canada on the implementation of CEDAW, the Committee expressed concern about *"the absence of a comprehensive national gender equality strategy, policy and action plan addressing the structural factors that cause persistent gender inequalities."* As a result, the Committee recommended that Canada *"develops a comprehensive national gender strategy, policy and action plan addressing the structural factors that cause persistent inequalities"* (United Nations, 2016[21]). Similar concerns regarding the absence of a national strategy were raised by civil society organisations[6] in reports submitted to the Committee (OXFAM Canada, 2017[22]); (Canadian Feminist Alliance for International Action (FAFIA), 2016[23]).

In the context of Canada's constitutional principles and federalism, a pan-Canadian strategy could entail a set of shared priorities, objectives and commonly agreed indicators on gender. A gender equality strategy could also roll out a governance structure and a common monitoring framework. It would recognise the prerogative of different levels of government to design their own policies while advancing shared priorities.

The development of a pan-Canadian gender equality strategy should draw upon examples of pan-Canadian strategies developed/being developed in other policy sectors such as environmental protection and early learning and childcare (see Box 1.4). Other recent examples include the Federal, Provincial and Territorial Declaration on Public Sector Innovation and the National Strategy for Financial Literacy.

Box 1.4. Examples of Pan-Canadian policy frameworks

Pan-Canadian Framework on Clean Growth and Climate Change

Over the coming year federal, provincial and territorial governments will work collaboratively through a new working group established under the Canadian Council of Ministers of the Environment and through innovation Ministers to identify and develop appropriate ways to measure progress in the Pan-Canadian Framework, including through use of indicators which draw on existing best practices. Future reports will also identify policy outcomes, track progress using indicators against objectives, and provide recommendations on new opportunities for collaboration or expanded areas of work.

The implementation of the Pan-Canadian Framework is a collaborative effort and shared responsibility of federal, provincial and territorial governments. A governance structure has been established to support intergovernmental coordination on Pan-Canadian Framework implementation and reporting. Nine FTP Ministerial Tables are responsible for coordinating Pan-Canadian Framework actions that fall within their respective Ministerial Portfolios.

A Federal-Provincial-Territorial Coordinating Committee of Experts has been established to develop the annual Synthesis Report to First Ministers that integrates Pan-Canadian Framework related input from the FTP Ministerial Tables.

The Intergovernmental Affairs Deputy Minister plays a key role in finalising and delivering this annual report to the First Ministers.

In order to avoid duplication with provincial and territorial reporting mechanisms, this work will build on existing climate change reporting across governments including drawing on existing indicators and best practices.

Multilateral Early Learning and Child Care Framework

On June 12, 2017, Federal, Provincial and Territorial Ministers Responsible for Early Learning and Child Care agreed to a Multilateral Early Learning and Child Care Framework. The new Framework sets the foundation for governments to work towards a shared long-term vision where all children across Canada can experience the enriching environment of quality early learning and child care. The guiding principles of the Framework are to increase quality, accessibility, affordability, flexibility and inclusivity in early learning and child care.

Governments are to work together, recognising that provinces and territories have the primary responsibility for the design and delivery of early learning and child care systems. Each provincial and territorial government determines its own priorities for early learning and child care and the Framework provides flexibility on how provinces and territories will meet objectives defined in the Framework.

Governments are to report annually on progress made in relation to the Framework and the impact of federal funding, while reflecting the priorities of each jurisdiction in early learning and child care.

Source: (Government of Canada, 2017[24])

Some civil society stakeholders noted that the 1967 Royal Commission on the Status of Women in Canada could provide a useful starting point for discussions around a pan-Canadian strategy for gender equality. The Royal Commission was established at a moment where women's rights issues were to the forefront nationally and internationally, and reflected a widespread sense of urgency to take action. Elements of the current international discourse on gender equality, and on empowerment of women and girls, are similarly in tune with the agenda of feminist reform within Canada. Against this background, it may be timely for the federal government to open a nation-wide dialogue about how gender inequality and inclusion can be addressed in a coordinated way.

Moving forward, in the context of Canada's stated commitment to gender equality and its results and delivery agenda, the OECD suggests that Canada builds on positive steps it has taken recently by establishing a Gender Results Framework, and use this framework as a foundation for:

- The development of an overarching gender equality strategy at the federal level, with specific targets, clear allocation of roles, resources and lines of accountability for the whole-of-government, and an accompanying implementation plan and a data strategy. "Anchoring" and aligning this strategy with the results and delivery agenda of the Government and each department (e.g. mandate letters, Results and Delivery Charters, departmental results frameworks) could maximise its effective implementation. (see Recommendation 9)
- Engagement with Federal, Provincial and Territorial Governments to work towards a pan-Canadian approach and strategy to gender equality, and to support Canada in implementing its international commitments such as CEDAW and SDGs. The impact of such an approach could be boosted by aligning policy objectives developed at Federal, Provincial and Territorial (FPT) levels, while respecting the autonomy and flexibility of FPT governments in designing their own policies.

This twin-tracked approach clarifies the overarching gender equality objectives for government as well as civil society and allows Canada to address gender inequalities from a holistic and people-centred perspective. This in turn helps improve policy prioritisation as well as transparency and accountability. There is also the potential for enhanced dialogue between the FPT levels of government, facilitating improved policy coherence and a platform to share good practices.

Notes

[1] OECD calculations based on official websites of Provincial and Territorial legislatures.

https://www.leg.bc.ca/wotv/pages/representation-today.aspx
http://www.legassembly.gov.yk.ca/members/index.html
http://www.ontla.on.ca/web/members/members_current.do?locale=en&ord=Riding&dir=ASC&list_type=all_mpps

https://www.assembly.ab.ca/lao/mla/SeatPlan.pdf

https://nslegislature.ca/members/profiles

http://www.assnat.qc.ca/en/deputes/

http://www.assembly.nu.ca/members/mla

http://www.legassembly.sk.ca/mlas/

https://gov.mb.ca/legislature/members/mla_list_alphabetical.html

http://www.assembly.pe.ca/current-members

http://www1.gnb.ca/legis/bios/58/index-e.asp

http://www.assembly.gov.nt.ca/members

http://www.swc-cfc.gc.ca/transition/tab_2_1-en.html

[2] OECD (2017), The *Pursuit of Gender Equality: An Uphill Battle*, OECD Publishing, Paris, http://dx.doi.org/10.1787/9789264281318-en

[3] http://www.canadabeyond150.ca/themes-methods-en.html

[4] The federal gender apparatus can be described as institutions, policies, tools and accountability structures to promote gender equality and mainstreaming at the federal level.

[5] Along with France, Iceland, Sweden and Slovenia

[6] Feminist Alliance for International Action highlights "*the need for a comprehensive plan is underscored by the fact that Canada has no national machinery for the advancement of women. Federal, provincial and territorial governments have different mechanisms; British Columbia has none, and some have assigned little authority or resources to this portfolio. Discussion among governments on women's equality issues takes place at meetings of Status of Women Ministers, but there is no formal co-ordination.*" OXFAM Canada also recommends *implementing the CEDAW Committee's 2016 recommendation for Canada to develop a comprehensive national gender equality strategy, policy and action plan that addresses the structural factors causing inequality.*

References

Andalusian Regional Government Administration (2014), *PROGRESS IN THE ANDALUSIAN GRB INITIATIVE: GENDER AUDITS*, https://www.wu.ac.at/fileadmin/wu/d/i/vw3/Session_3_Cirujano_Gualda_Romero.pdf (accessed on 17 May 2018). [54]

Australian Government((n.d.)), *National Women's Alliances | Department of the Prime Minister and Cabinet*, 2018, https://www.pmc.gov.au/office-women/grants-and-funding/national-womens-alliances (accessed on 17 May 2018). [48]

Batliwala, S., S. Rosenhek and J. Miller (2013), "WOMEN MOVING MOUNTAINS: COLLECTIVE IMPACT OF THE DUTCH MDG3 FUND HOW RESOURCES ADVANCE WOMEN'S RIGHTS AND GENDER EQUALITY", https://www.awid.org/sites/default/files/atoms/files/Women%20Moving%20Mountains.pdf. [46]

Bochel, H. and A. Berthier (2018), *SPICe Briefing: Committee witnesses: gender and representation*, https://sp-bpr-en-prod-cdnep.azureedge.net/published/2018/2/27/Committee-witnesses--gender-and-representation/SB%2018-16.pdf (accessed on 17 May 2018). [52]

Bohnet, I. (2016), *What works: Gender Equality by Design*, Harvard University Press. [16]

Canadian Feminist Alliance for International Action (FAFIA) (2016), *Because its 2016! A National Gender Equality Plan*, http://tbinternet.ohchr.org/Treaties/CEDAW/Shared%20Documents/CAN/INT_CEDAW_NGO [23]

_CAN_25417_E.pdf (accessed on 12 December 2017).

Canadian Institute for Advanced Research & Vancouver School of Economics (2016), *Earnings Inequality and the Gender Pay Gap*, http://faculty.arts.ubc.ca/nfortin/Fortin_EarningsInequalityGenderPayGap.pdf. [6]

Catalyst (2017), *Women In Male-Dominated Industries And Occupations*, http://www.catalyst.org/knowledge/women-male-dominated-industries-and-occupations. [10]

Congressional Budget Office (2016), *CBO's 2016 Long-Term Projections for Social Security: Additional Information*, https://www.cbo.gov/sites/default/files/114th-congress-2015-2016/reports/52298-socialsecuritychartbook.pdf. [62]

Downes, R., L. Von Trapp and S. Nicol (2016), "Gender budgeting in OECD countries", *OECD Journal on Budgeting* 3, http://www.oecd.org/gender/Gender-Budgeting-in-OECD-countries.pdf. [59]

EIGE (2018), *Spain – Structures*, http://eige.europa.eu/gender-mainstreaming/countries/spain/structures. [27]

European Parliament (2016), *Report on Gender Mainstreaming in the work of the European Parliament - A8-0034/2016*, http://www.europarl.europa.eu/sides/getDoc.do?type=REPORT&reference=A8-2016-0034&language=EN (accessed on 17 May 2018). [51]

European Parliament (2003), *European Parliament resolution on gender mainstreaming in the European Parliament (2002/2025(INI))*, http://www.europarl.europa.eu/sides/getDoc.do?pubRef=-//EP//TEXT+TA+P5-TA-2003-0098+0+DOC+XML+V0//EN. [50]

Flumian, M. (2016), "What Trudeau's committees tell us about his government | Institute on Governance", *Institute on Governance*, https://iog.ca/research-publications/publications/what-trudeaus-committees-tell-us-about-his-government/ (accessed on 21 January 2018). [29]

Goldin, C. (2014), "A Grand Gender Convergence: Its Last Chapter", *American Economic Review*, Vol. 104/4, pp. 1091-1119. [5]

Government of Canada (2018), *Budget 2018: Equality + Growth, A Strong Middle Class*, https://www.budget.gc.ca/2018/docs/plan/budget-2018-en.pdf. [8]

Government of Canada (2018), *Budget Plan + Growth*, https://financebudget.azurewebsites.net/2018/docs/plan/chap-01-en.html?wbdisable=true. [7]

Government of Canada (2018), *Innovation, Science and Economic Development Canada - Canada.ca*, https://www.canada.ca/en/innovation-science-economic-development.html. [44]

Government of Canada (2018), *Mandate Letter Tracker: Delivering results for Canadians*, https://www.canada.ca/en/privy-council/campaigns/mandate-tracker-results-canadians.html (accessed on 10 February 2018). [33]

Government of Canada (2018), *Policy on Results*, https://www.tbs-sct.gc.ca/pol/doc-eng.aspx?id=31300 (accessed on 17 May 2018). [38]

Government of Canada (2017), *Budget 2017: Building a Strong Middle Class*, https://www.budget.gc.ca/2017/docs/plan/budget-2017-en.pdf. [57]

Government of Canada (2017), *Fact Sheet: It's time to pay attention*, http://www.swc-cfc.gc.ca/violence/strategy-strategie/fs-fi-3-en.html. [45]

Government of Canada (2017), *Multilateral Early Learning and Child Care Framework - Canada.ca*, https://www.canada.ca/en/employment-social-development/programs/early-learning-child-care/reports/2017-multilateral-framework.html (accessed on 11 December 2017). [24]

Government of Canada (2017), *Results and Delivery in Canada: Building on momentum*, http://www.fmi.ca/media/1200856/results_and_delivery_building_momentum_october_2017.pdf. [34]

Government of Canada (2016), *Fall Economic Statement 2016*, https://www.budget.gc.ca/fes-eea/2016/docs/statement-enonce/fes-eea-2016-eng.pdf. [56]

Government of Canada (2016), *Increasing Recruitment of Women into the Canadian Armed Forces*. [17]

Government of Canada((n.d.)), *Charter Statements - Canada's System of Justice*, 2018, http://www.justice.gc.ca/eng/csj-sjc/pl/charter-charte/index.html (accessed on 17 May 2018). [41]

Government of Canada((n.d.)), *Employment Insurance Service Quality Review Report: Making Citizens Central*, 2017, https://www.canada.ca/en/employment-social-development/programs/ei/ei-list/reports/service-quality-review-report.html. [43]

Government of Finland (2016), *Government Action Plan For Gender Equality 2016–2019*, https://julkaisut.valtioneuvosto.fi/bitstream/handle/10024/79305/03_2017_Tasa-arvo-ohjelma_Enkku_kansilla.pdf?sequence=1. [19]

Government of Iceland((n.d.)), *Gender Budgeting*, 2018, https://www.government.is/topics/economic-affairs-and-public-finances/gender-budgeting/ (accessed on 16 May 2018). [60]

Government of Spain (2014), *Plan Estratégico de Igualdad de Oportunidades 2014-2016*, http://www.inmujer.gob.es/actualidad/PEIO/docs/PEIO2014-2016.pdf. [20]

Government of Sweden (2014), *Sweden's follow-up of the Platform for Action from the UN's*, https://www.regeringen.se/contentassets/b2f5cc340526433f8e33df3024d510e3/swedens-follow-up-of-the-platform-for-action-from-the-uns-fourth-world-conference-on-women-in-beijing-1995---covering-the-period-between-20092014. [47]

Government of Sweden (2007), *Moving Ahead: Gender budgeting in Sweden*, http://store1.digitalcity.eu.com/store/clients/release/AAAAGNJH/doc/gender-budgeting-in-sweden_2007.09.29-12.22.48.pdf. [65]

House of Commons Canada (2008), *Committee Report No. 9 - FEWO (39-2) - House of Commons of Canada*, http://www.ourcommons.ca/DocumentViewer/en/39-2/FEWO/report-9/. [53]

House of Commons Canada (2007), *Report of the Standing Committee on the Status of Women: The impacts of funding and program changes at Status of Women Canada*, http://www.ourcommons.ca/Content/Committee/391/FEWO/Reports/RP2876038/feworp18/feworp18-e.pdf (accessed on 23 January 2018). [26]

House of Commons Canada((n.d.)), *FEWO - About*, 2018, https://www.ourcommons.ca/Committees/en/FEWO/About (accessed on 17 May 2018). [49]

IMF (2017), *Gender Budgeting in G7 Countries*, https://www.imf.org/en/Publications/Policy-Papers/Issues/2017/05/12/pp041917gender-budgeting-in-g7-countries. [36]

Mahony, T. (2011), "Women and the Criminal Justice System", *Statistics Canada Catalogue no. 89-503-X*, http://www.statcan.gc.ca/pub/89-503-x/2010001/article/11416-eng.pdf (accessed on 17 May 2018). [11]

McInturff, K. and B. Lambert (2016), *Making Women Count: The Unequal Economics of Women's Work*, | Canadian Centre for Policy Alternatives, OXFAM Canada, https://www.policyalternatives.ca/publications/reports/making-women-count-0 (accessed on 01 January 2018). [13]

McKinsey Global Institute (2017), *The power of parity: Advancing women's equality in Canada*, https://www.mckinsey.com/featured-insights/gender-equality/the-power-of-parity-advancing-womens-equality-in-canada (accessed on 16 May 2018). [2]

Moyser, M. (2017), *Women and Paid Work, Statistics Canada, March, available online at: http://www.statcan.gc.ca/pub/89-503-x/2015001/article/14694-eng.htm.* [4]

OECD (2017), *Behavioural Insights and Public Policy: Lessons from Around the World.*, OECD Publishing. [15]

OECD (2017), *Building an inclusive Mexico : Policies and Good Governance for Gender Equality*, OECD Publishing. [28]

OECD (2017), *Recommendation of the Council on Open Government*, http://www.oecd.org/gov/Recommendation-Open-Government-Approved-Council-141217.pdf. [42]

OECD (2017), *The Pursuit of Gender Equality: An Uphill Battle*, OECD Publishing, Paris, http://dx.doi.org/10.1787/9789264281318-en. [1]

OECD (2016), *Open Government The Global Context and the Way Forward*, OECD Publishing. [32]

OECD (2016), "Open Government: The Global Context and The Way Forward", http://www.oecd-ilibrary.org/docserver/download/4216481e.pdf?expires=1516890637&id=id&accname=ocid84004878&checksum=36020513E75CAF56257B41F9DC2A3AFC (accessed on 25 January 2018). [31]

OECD (2015), "Delivering from the Centre: Strengthening the role of the centre of government in driving priority strategies", https://www.oecd.org/gov/cog-2015-delivering-priority- [25]

strategies.pdf (accessed on 21 January 2018).

OECD (Forthcoming), *Budgeting in Austria.* [37]

OECD (Forthcoming), *Budgeting Outlook 2018.* [39]

OECD (Forthcoming), *Budgeting Practices and Procedures Dataset.* [58]

OECD (Forthcoming), *Governance Guidelines for Gender Budgeting.* [64]

OECD (forthcoming) (2018), *OECD Economic Surveys: Canada, OECD Publishing, Paris.* [3]

Office of the Auditor General Canada (2016), *Implementing Gender-Based Analysis*, http://www.oag-bvg.gc.ca/internet/English/parl_oag_201602_01_e_41058.html (accessed on 24 January 2018). [30]

Office of the Auditor General of Canada((n.d.)), *The Environment and Sustainable Development Guide*, 2018, http://www.oag-bvg.gc.ca/internet/English/meth_lp_e_19275.html (accessed on 17 May 2018). [55]

OXFAM Canada (2017), *Feminist Scorecard 2017: Tracking government action to advance women's rights and gender equality*, http://www.oxfam.ca (accessed on 11 December 2017). [22]

Schratzenstaller, M. (2014), *The implementation of gender responsive budgeting in Austria as central element of a major budget reform*, https://www.wu.ac.at/fileadmin/wu/d/i/vw3/Session_4_Schratzenstaller.pdf. [35]

Sharp, R. and R. Broomhill (2013), *A Case Study of Gender Responsive Budgeting in Australia*, https://consultations.worldbank.org/Data/hub/files/grb_papers_australia_updf_final.pdf. [63]

Status of Women Canada (2017), *It's Time: Canada's Strategy To Prevent and Address Gender-based Violence*, Government of Canada, http://www.swc-cfc.gc.ca/violence/strategy-strategie/GBV_Fact_sheets_2.pdf (accessed on 01 January 2018). [12]

Status of Women Canada((n.d.)), *The History of GBA+ Domestic and International Milestones.* [14]

Swedish Fiscal Policy Council (2016), *Finanspolitiska rådets rapport 2016*, http://www.finanspolitiskaradet.com/download/18.21a8337f154abc1a5dd28c15/1463487699296/Svensk+finanspolitik+2016.pdf. [61]

The Victorian Government (2018), *Safe and Strong: A Victorian Gender Equality Strategy. Achievements Report Year One*, https://www.vic.gov.au/system/user_files/Documents/women/1801009_Safe_and_strong_first_year_report_summary_10_%C6%92_web.pdf (accessed on 17 May 2018). [18]

UK National Audit Office (2016), *Sustainability in the spending review*, https://www.nao.org.uk/wp-content/uploads/2016/07/Sustainability-in-the-Spending-Review.pdf. [40]

United Nations (2016), "Concluding observations on the combined eighth and ninth periodic [21] reports of Canada*", https://documents-dds-ny.un.org/doc/UNDOC/GEN/N16/402/03/PDF/N1640203.pdf?OpenElement (accessed on 11 December 2017).

Wells, M. (2018), *Closing the Engineering Gender Gap*, https://www.design-engineering.com/features/engineering-gender-gap/. [9]

Chapter 2. Canada's institutional approach to gender equality

This chapter considers Canada's institutional design for gender mainstreaming from a whole-of-government perspective by assessing the roles and responsibilities of Status of Women Canada (SWC), the centre of government, federal departments and Statistics Canada in delivering Gender Based Analysis Plus (GBA+) and gender budgeting commitments. It also discusses horizontal coordination structures such as the Cabinet Committee on Diversity and Inclusion, and modalities of collaboration between the Federal Government, Provinces and Territories. Canada's institutional design is well advanced in international terms and is broadly in line with the 2015 Recommendation. To further boost SWC's position as an institutional champion, consideration could be given to modernise its mandate to encompass gender equality and related dimensions of equality and inclusion. Further reinforcement of the challenge function of the centre of government would allow for more effective quality control and impact assessment of GBA+ and gender budgeting.

2.1. Introduction

Canada has a strong whole-of-government institutional framework for gender (plus) mainstreaming at the federal level (see Box 2.1). Encompassing clear roles for a federal agency (Status of Women Canada), the centre of government, departments and other bodies, as well as independent oversight, this comprehensive institutional approach is in line with the 2015 Recommendation and, in many respects, represents advanced international practice.

Canada's institutional design for gender mainstreaming refers to:

- A federal gender institution **(Status of Women Canada)** tasked with leading and facilitating a system-wide response to gender equality gaps and needs;
- Steering and leadership from the Centre of Government **(Privy Council Office, Treasury Board Secretariat, Department of Finance)** to support and challenge the administration in its implementation of gender mainstreaming;
- Clearly assigned roles and responsibilities within **departments** to implement gender mainstreaming as a shared responsibility;
- The body that collects and produces data **(Statistics Canada)** to ensure high-quality gender-disaggregated evidence is available to support decision-making;
- **Co-ordination** structures and tools (e.g., IT) that ensure policy coherence for gender equality at all levels such as the Network for GBA+ champions; and
- Accountability from the legislature, independent institutions (**Parliament, Parliamentary Budget Office, Office of the Auditor General**), and civil society.

This chapter provides a detailed examination of this institutional framework and proposes recommendations to enhance its effectiveness and impact.

Figure 2.1. Institutional design for gender mainstreaming at the federal level in Canada

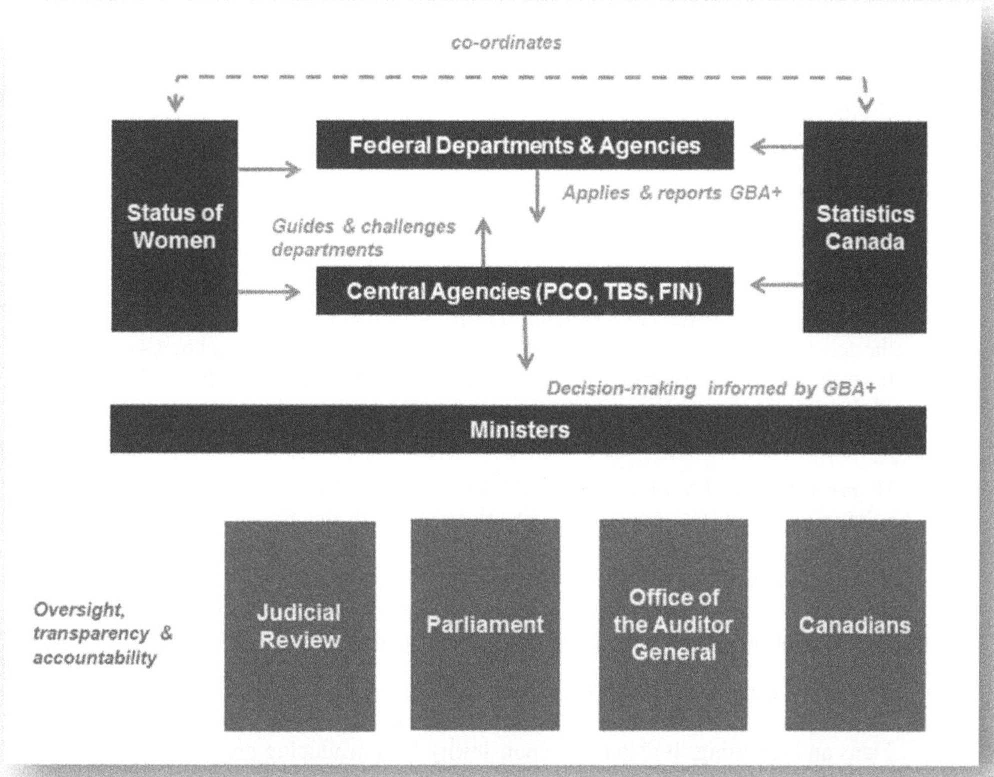

Source: OECD

Box 2.1. An overview of institutional roles and responsibilities for gender equality

Federal administration:

- **Status of Women Canada** is the institution responsible for leading key policy initiatives on issues affecting women and girls. It is also tasked with providing expert advice across the federal government on women's equality issues; and leading the Government's implementation of GBA+ through building capacity and advice.

Central agencies:

Working to achieve substantial gender equality is a complex, cross-cutting, multidimensional exercise. It requires the involvement of and buy-in from all government actors and beyond. Across OECD countries, the Centre of Government (CoG) is uniquely placed to ensure such buy-in across the government. Given its convening and steering functions in driving policy priorities (OECD, 2015[25]), the CoG also plays a key role in the governance of gender equality work.

Firstly, the central agencies can support the effective implementation of gender mainstreaming tools by clarifying expectations throughout the administration and providing a challenge function to ensure that such tools are used to inform policy and budget decisions. Secondly, the CoG – together with the gender institution – can promote a strategic vision and roadmap for the administration to deliver on its gender equality commitments. The important role of central agencies is also highlighted by the OECD Toolkit for Gender Equality in Governance.

In Canada, In 2016, when GBA+ became a mandatory assessment for all policy proposals brought before Cabinet, the quality-assurance function of these central agencies has been strengthened. As GBA+ does not have a legislative underpinning, the leadership from the central agencies has proven crucial to engage federal departments in gender mainstreaming efforts.

Detail on the individual roles of each of the central agencies is provided in the following paragraphs.

- **Privy Council Office (PCO)** supports the implementation of GBA+ throughout the federal government. The PCO requires all departments and agencies consider the application of GBA+ in the development of memoranda to Cabinet (MCs) and challenges departments on the use of GBA+ through the normal policy development process.
- **Department of Finance (FIN)** has the mandate to develop and implement economic, fiscal, tax, social, security, international and financial sector policies and programmes, and to prepare federal budget. It is also responsible for leading the implementation of gender budgeting. Since 2016, FIN has led on the development of gender budgeting as a tool of gender mainstreaming. The Department published Canada's first gender statement as part of Budget 2017.
- **Treasury Board Secretariat (TBS)** ensures GBA+ is incorporated into the Treasury Board Submissions, Departmental Results Frameworks, Departmental Plans and reporting. It also has responsibility for introducing gender policies such as proactive pay equity legislation for federally-regulated workers, strategies to combat sexual harassment in federal public institutions and for increasing the number of women in senior decision-making positions across government.
- **Statistics Canada:** provides gender-disaggregated data through its surveys; and facilitates instituting a GBA+ research framework. It also publishes numerous analytical reports using gender-disaggregated data and intersecting identities, including the "Women in Canada" series.
- **Federal departments and agencies** are given the shared responsibility to conduct gender-based analysis and report on its outcomes.

Mechanisms for policy direction and co-ordination at the federal level:

- **Deputy Ministers Task Force for Diversity and Inclusion** examines and formulates advice on how to promote inclusion, to ensure Canada fully benefits from the participation of all Canadians in our economic, social, cultural, and civic life.
- **Network of GBA+ champions** seeks to engage senior officials appointed as GBA+ Champions for the implementation of GBA+ in their department or agency. The network seeks to encourage collaboration and support, and to share strategies and best practices on how to "champion" sustainable GBA+ practices.
- **The InterDepartmental Committee (IDC)** serves to facilitate a common understanding of GBA+ and to support its sustainable practice in the federal government. The IDC's activities aim to increase the federal government's GBA+ capacity and expertise; provide a forum for sharing information and best

practices; and promote collaboration amongst members to develop GBA+ tools, resources and training.

- **Public Service Management Advisory Committee** provides a forum for discussion of the public service management agenda. GBA+ is discussed at this committee once per year.

Accountability structures:

- **Office of the Auditor General** serves Parliament by providing it with objective, fact-based information and expert advice on GBA+, gathered through audits. The latest report of the Auditor General on GBA+ was released in fall 2015.
- **Status of Women Committee (FEWO) Parliamentary Committee:** The House of Commons may refer certain matters to the House of Commons Standing Committee on the Status of Women for examination and report. The Committee has broad authority to study policies, programmes, expenditures (budgetary estimates) and legislation of departments and agencies, including Status of Women Canada; and to create subcommittees to focus on particular subjects.
- **Human Rights Committee in the Senate** studies issues relating to human rights and reviews the machinery of government dealing with Canada's international and national human rights obligations including on gender equality.
- **General Courts and Supreme Court of Canada** enforce the Canadian Charter of Rights and Freedoms containing guaranteed equality rights; and the Canadian Human Rights Act prohibiting gender-based discrimination. The Supreme Court of Canada also acts as the final arbiter and contributes to the development of all branches of law applicable within Canada.

Multi-level governance and co-ordination:

- **The Federal/Provincial/Territorial Ministers (FPT) Responsible for the Status of Women:** Provincial and territorial governments are in charge of gender equality policies under their jurisdictions. The Federal/Provincial/Territorial Ministers (FPT) Responsible for the Status of Women, an intergovernmental body, acts as a coordination mechanism between the federal and provincial/territorial levels. It meets annually to share information, exchange best practices and explore issues that affect Canadian women and girls including violence against women and girls, women's economic security, and women in leadership.

2.2. Federal roles and responsibilities to improve gender equality outcomes

2.2.1. Status of Women Canada (SWC)

A number of agencies and departments in the federal government of Canada are responsible for issues related to different aspects of diversity and inclusion. According to the Heritage Act, the advancement of diversity and inclusion has been a core responsibility of the Department of Canadian Heritage. Its mandate includes promoting multiculturalism, human rights, Indigenous languages & cultures, and youth engagement. With the increased focus of the government on diversity and inclusion, the Privy Council Office (PCO) established an LGBTQ2 Secretariat within its Social Policy Development Unit, although its sustainability depends on continued political will. The youth engagement policy has also been addressed by the centre of government. PCO's Results and Delivery Unit is also working to establish a Diversity and Inclusion Charter with related indicators for the administration to measure progress. However, PCO's primary focus in this area has been achieving more diverse and inclusive workforce within the federal public administration. Immigration, Refugees and Citizenship Canada is another federal department that works to advance diversity and inclusion. In parallel, according to its current mandate, Status of Women Canada (SWC) is the institution responsible for leading key policy initiatives on issues affecting women and girls. It is also tasked with providing expert advice across the federal government on women's equality issues; and leading the Government's implementation of GBA+ through building capacity and advice. Section 2.2.2 below considers the need for a co-ordinated approach to address diversity and inclusion agenda, including but also beyond gender equality.

The strong political focus on gender equality, diversity and inclusion has significantly boosted the role and influence of SWC. The federal departments and agencies are increasingly seeking SWC support for the implementation of GBA+. There is also increased coordination between SWC and the central agencies regarding the identification of overarching gender equality objectives and implementation of GBA+. These developments tend to support a well-functioning and impactful gender apparatus, and are consistent with the 2015 Recommendation.

Further clarifying and scaling up the mandate of SWC can provide a strong institutional champion to drive gender equality beyond women's status, with increasing attention to intersecting identity factors within policy making. Some areas can be identified, drawing upon the OECD Toolkit for Mainstreaming and Implementing Gender Equality, where specific improvements would be likely to have most impact in Canada.

- While there is no blueprint for the institutional design for gender equality bodies across the OECD (see examples in Box 2.2 and Box 2.3), their level of responsibility and position within the governmental structure are indicative of their effectiveness (see Figure 2.2). From its inception, SWC was given the mandate to "coordinate policy with respect to the status of women and administer related programmes". This mandate was not matched with full representation in the Cabinet, a factor which appears, at times, to have constrained the political influence of SWC throughout various administrations. These challenges are also recognised by the Committee on the Elimination of Discrimination against Women (United Nations, 2016[21]). Moreover, the OECD notes that many stakeholders, both within public administration and in civil society, retain a perception of SWC as an agency responsible for administering women's programmes, as distinct from an agency responsible for developing and coordinating a consistent federal response to gender equality needs across the country.

Figure 2.2. Central gender institutions in OECD countries, 2017

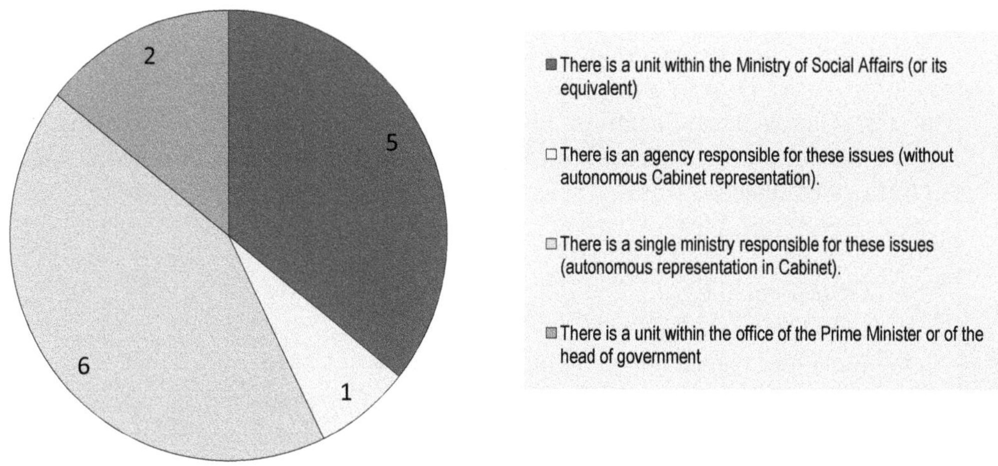

Source: 2017 OECD Survey on National Gender Equality Frameworks and Public Policies (preliminary results)

- Having the sufficient mandate and resources for promoting gender equality and supporting a government-wide gender equality policy are also indicative of the effectiveness of gender equality institutions. Historically, SWC has experienced significant reductions in its operating budget and mandate (House of Commons Canada, 2007[26]), although its budget has been increased in recent years in keeping with its enhanced profile, and with the renewed government commitment to GBA+.
- Transparency of GBA+ and timeframes provided for policy analysis and consultation are another set of areas where further improvements can significantly boost the impact of SWC with an increased and timely access to gender (plus) analysis by the departments (Chapter 3). While there is no formal requirement for federal departments to consult SWC, the latter is increasingly sought by the departments since GBA+ became a mandatory requirement. In the current setting, however, the departments tend to engage SWC at the late stages of policy planning, thus limiting the influence of gender analysis on the decision-making process.

There is an accelerated momentum in Canada to address these challenges, and to reinforce the authority and mandate of SWC in a way that it is enduring into the future. Some steps are already taken in this regard and the most important one include the appointment of the first-ever full Minister of Status of Women in November 2015. The Government's renewed commitment to GBA+ as reflected in the GBA+ Action Plan for 2016-2020 has also strengthened the mandate of SWC as the "go-to institution" in ensuring government policy, legislation, and regulations are sensitive to the different impacts that decisions have on men and women. Resources of SWC have been increased accordingly. Since SWC started monitoring the federal implementation of GBA+ through a Deputy Ministers Survey, an increasing number of departments are making the GBA+ training mandatory for some or all employees. Most recently, in alignment with the preliminary discussions between the Government of Canada and the OECD in the context of this Review, Budget 2018 committed to making SWC an official Department of the

Government of Canada by introducing departmental legislation to solidify the roles of SWC and its Minister.

Box 2.2. The United Kingdom Government Equalities Office

The UK Government Equalities Office (GEO) operates across Government and is responsible for promoting equality for women and lesbian, gay, bisexual & transgender (LGBT) individuals.

GEO is responsible for:

- Gender equality
- LGBT equality
- Equalities legislation including the Equality Act 2010
- Sponsoring the Equality and Human Rights Commission
- Other government departments are responsible for policy around:
- Race
- Disability
- Age
- Religion
- Pregnancy & maternity

GEO works closely with other government departments to deliver its priorities, maintain the equalities framework, and promote equality. It also works with a range of stakeholders external to government, including businesses, third sector organisations, and academics.

GEO's commitments include:

- Take measures to close the gender pay gap
- Continue to work for parity in the number of public appointments going to women
- Increase female representation on FTSE 350 boards to 33% by 2020
- Publish a response to the findings of the national LGBT survey
- Consult on reforms to the Gender Recognition Act in order to streamline and de-medicalise the legal gender recognition process
- Carry out an internal review of gender markers in official documents
- Track commitments made in response to the Women and Equalities Select Committee reports, and respond to future inquiries

Source: UK Government Equalities Office 2018

Box 2.3. The Women's Institutes of Spain and Mexico

Spain

The Women's Institute of Spain was created under Law 16/1983 of 24 October as an autonomous body and the first governmental structure devoted specifically to foster gender equality (EIGE 2018). Article 2 of the law established that the Institute's primary mandate was to promote conditions that favour true equality between men and women and the government later charged the Institute with the mandate to elaborate a plan to promote equality. The Institute is now affiliated to the Directorate General of Equal Opportunities and includes two observatories: the Observatory for Equal Opportunities between Men and Women, which reviews and assesses gender gaps in socio-economic life and makes policy proposals to protect and improve women's rights; and the Observatory of Women's Image, created in 1994 to foster attitudinal change by promoting a non-stereotyped image of women (EIGE 2018). Additionally, ten autonomous communities in Spain have independent agencies comparable to the Women's Institute at the national level, which are institutionalised by law and have their own budget and staff and similar goals and tasks (EIGE 2018).

Sources: (EIGE, 2018[27])

Mexico

The federal Government of Mexico has developed an elaborated legal framework to advance gender equality and mainstreaming. The 2001 Law of the National Women's Institute establishes INMUJERES as an autonomous body that acts as central gender institution and has as its objectives to promote women's rights, to coordinate, monitor and evaluate gender equality policies, to promote a non-violent and non-discriminatory culture and to monitor compliance with international treaties. The 2006 General Act on Equality between Women and Men lays out a blueprint for building a gender-equality framework (both across government and at the secretariat level). It establishes three national policy instruments: the National System for Equality, the National Programme for Equality and the Observance. The Equality Act devotes specific chapters to the roles of all parties engaged in implementation of gender equality policies, from federal government to states and municipalities.

Source: (OECD, 2017[28])

Scaling up the mandate of Status of Women Canada

Looking ahead, SWC's role as the lead institution responsible for coordinating and facilitating the implementation of gender equality policy should be strengthened, if the on-going reform process is to be maintained and reinforced. In the context of formalising SWC as an official department, consideration could be given to scaling up the mandate to expand the focus from solely women and include the focus on broader issues related to gender equality, and align with the broad nature of Gender-based Analysis Plus (GBA+). This, together with the appropriate resourcing, could help SWC to become the government's policy hub and "go-to institution" on issues of gender equality and intersecting identity factors. In addition, stronger collaboration between SWC, central agencies and Statistics Canada can ensure that gender equality (plus) is systematically considered in departmental policy development and cascades through the results and delivery framework.

2.2.2. The Cabinet and the Minister of Status of Women

In Canada, the Cabinet is the centre of political decision making. The representation of gender equality issues within the Cabinet is important for the gender equality (plus) agenda to become embedded in the daily work of the federal administration.

The top-level political commitment to gender equality, diversity and inclusion in Canada has resulted in three major initiatives which increase the visibility of gender equality questions at Cabinet.

- Firstly, providing the Minister of Status of Women with a full-fledged representation in the Cabinet process has been an important step in implementing the Government of Canada's pledge to gender equality. The Cabinet is organised in form of Committees that are in charge of bringing government's agenda to fruition in their own areas of responsibility. The Minister of Status of Women is currently a member of three Cabinet Committees (CCs) including the CC on Diversity and Inclusion; the CC on Open Transparent Government and Parliament; and the CC on Growing the Middle Class. The Minister is also an alternate member of the Treasury Board which acts as the government's management board and provides oversight on financial management, spending and human resources.
- Secondly, making GBA+ mandatory for all Cabinet submissions has created an opportunity for gender equality considerations to be regularly discussed in all Cabinet Committees.
- Thirdly, the Cabinet committees set the tone of the government and signal top-level priorities (Flumian, 2016[29]). Accordingly, a small but increasing number of OECD countries are establishing structures to deal with gender equality issues at the Cabinet level (see Box 2.4 for the example of Iceland). In Canada, the creation of the Cabinet Committee on Diversity and Inclusion (CCDI) sent a strong political signal about the importance of this agenda for the government.

Moving forward, there is room to maximise the impact of these initiatives by providing a more explicit mandate to one or more of the Cabinet Committees to work on gender equality. The mandate of the CCDI is to "*examine initiatives designed to strengthen the relationship with Indigenous Canadians, improve the economic performance of immigrants, and promote Canadian diversity, multiculturalism, and linguistic duality*". However, gender equality is not at the centre of the CCDI's mandate, and therefore the opportunities are not fully tapped for a Cabinet committee level engagement with important issues of deeply rooted gender stereotypes and multi-factorial discrimination associated with intersecting identity factors. There is scope for clarifying and focusing the mandate for the CCDI, allowing it to address more regularly and substantively the issue of gender equality both in its own right, and as a matter of intersectionality and inclusion.

Box 2.4. Ministerial Committee on Equality in Iceland

In 2017, with the renewed political commitment to gender equality in Iceland, the Prime Minister of Iceland and the Cabinet re-established the Ministerial Committee on Equality. The main role of the Committee is to coordinate equality issues among ministers and within the government. These issues include, but are not limited to, parental leave (paternity and maternity leave); the elimination of the gender pay gap (implementation of the law on the Equal Pay Standard); the rights of LGBTQ+ people; combating sexual violence; and ratification of the Istanbul Convention. The Ministers represented on the Committee are the Prime Minister; the Minister of Social Affairs and Equality; the Minister of Justice; the Minister of Health; and the Minister of Education and Culture. Other ministers participate in the meetings of the Committee on the basis of need and in accordance with the decision of the Prime Minister who chairs the meeting of the Committee.

Source: Government of Iceland 2018

There are other mechanisms at the Deputy Minister level for gender equality issues to be discussed. Notably, the Clerk of the Privy Council established a Task Force on Diversity and Inclusion (Task Force) co-chaired by the Deputy Ministers of Status of Women Canada and Immigration, Refugees and Citizenship Canada. Historically, task forces led by Deputy Ministers are mandated to explore a range of important and cross-cutting policy issues. The official mandate of this Task Force is to examine and formulate advice on how to promote inclusion, and to ensure Canada fully benefits from the participation of all Canadians in economic, social, cultural and civic life. Stemming from this broad mandate, the Task Force also works to formulate advice on how to advance a feminist government. The recommendations of the Task Force are planned to be formulated by summer 2018. Looking ahead, an important role for this Task Force could be to advance reflection on strengthening a coordinated federal response to gender equality, diversity and inclusion needs that are currently being addressed by a number of departments and agencies (e.g., SWC; Department of Canadian Heritage; PCO; Immigration, Refugees and Citizenship Canada).

Another platform for discussion about gender equality issues at the Deputy Minister level is the Public Service Management Advisory Committee (PSMAC) led by the Secretary of the Treasury Board. In the framework of the Gender-based Analysis Action Plan (2016-2020), PSMAC provides a platform once a year to discuss the government wide implementation of gender-based analysis. Engagement of senior management in gender mainstreaming has been proven crucial across OECD for such tools to take root and its importance is strongly stressed by the 2015 Recommendation. Therefore, Canada must be commended for achieving such high-level engagement across the federal administration, and encouraged to further institutionalise such platforms. However, early signals point that PSMAC do not provide a platform for substantial discussion about gender equality. Moving forward, it will be beneficial to complement such process and management oriented discussions with a higher level platform for discussion about society-wide gender equality goals and targets (see Chapter 1). Cabinet Committee and Deputy Ministers Task Force on Diversity and Inclusion provide a strong basis to kick-start these discussions.

Having a strong Cabinet representation and mandate is significant for gender equality and intersectionality issues to remain at the top of the political agenda. It also sends strong signals to the administration about the importance of this topic. However, additional delivery mechanisms are needed to address complex gender equality challenges. A growing body of evidence from OECD points to various challenges of having inter-ministerial mechanisms as the primary tool to resolve policy delivery issues. Given such structures are highly procedural and time sensitive, there is usually limited room for detailed discussion or data analysis (OECD, 2015[25]). To ensure a well-functioning institutional framework for gender equality in Canada, it will be equally important to work in parallel on consolidating and strengthening the roles and responsibilities across the administration (e.g., Centre of Government, Status of Women Canada, federal departments, etc.) to provide solid evidence-base and deliver on government's top commitments.

2.2.3. Centre of Government

The Canadian approach provides a good practice example of Centre of Government (CoG) involvement in gender equality governance (refer back to Box 2.1 for an overview of CoG roles and responsibilities). According to the current distribution of roles, central agencies (PCO, TBS, and FIN) provide a "gatekeeper" function, in ensuring that requirements in relation to gender-based policy analysis are upheld, as well as a "challenge" function with regard to the questions of analytical rigour and quality. In this context, the role of GBA+ as an integral element of Canada's policy making system and of the Policy on Results is increasingly important (see Chapter 3).

While the overall roles and responsibilities in central agencies for gender mainstreaming seem well allocated, there are a number of areas on the implementation side where further reinforcement will be beneficial to maximise the impact of on-going GBA+ and gender-budgeting initiatives. The following chapter will assess how the overall institutional framework can be boosted to allow for a quality control and impact assessment of gender-based analysis (Chapter 3). A particular shortcoming highlighted by the Office of the Auditor General has been the limited human resources capacity and knowledge within central agencies to exercise a meaningful challenge function (Office of the Auditor General Canada, 2016[30]). The GBA+ Action Plan 2016-2020 sets out the response of the Canadian federal administration aimed at addressing these shortcomings.

In the context of Budget 2018's commitment to introduce new GBA+ legislation, there is an opportunity to strengthen the challenge function of the central agencies by putting forward criteria for assessing the quality of GBA+ (see Chapter 3). In addition, in the context of the newly established Gender Results Framework (GRF), there is scope to identify clear roles and responsibilities for the central agencies for its implementation and accountability. Given its advisory role to the Prime Minister and the Cabinet in the implementation of government's priorities, PCO seems well placed to take on such role – in close collaboration with the other central agencies and with SWC.

2.2.4. Department of Justice

The functions of the Department of Justice (JUS) include providing legal advice, supporting the Crown in litigation, and policy-making. In its legal advisory role, the Department helps federal departments develop, reform, and interpret laws. In the preparation of draft bills, federal departments work with JUS generally from the early stages of the work. JUS continues to be involved in each step from obtaining Cabinet approval to drafting – and redrafting – the bill until it is enacted by Parliament. While JUS is not formally considered a central agency, it can play a central role in ensuring that all bills integrate a GBA+.

JUS has a GBA+ Unit since 2009 which is providing GBA+ advice and guidance to all employees, especially with respect to meeting the GBA+ requirements set out by the central agencies. With the increased political attention to gender equality, there is a greater integration of gender lens within the Department's work. In 2016, JUS sponsored a legislation to add gender identity as a prohibited ground for discrimination under the Canadian Human Rights Acts (Bill C-16). The Bill passed the legislative process and became law in 2017. Moving forward, JUS has a strong potential to play an increasingly active role in supporting a gender lens within legislative initiatives. In 2018, JUS updated its "Common Consideration Checklist" which is a tool to assist JUS officials to more easily and systematically fulfil high-level instructions that call for routine consideration of specific kinds of issues or implications, including gender equality. While the Checklist is not mandatory, completed checklists help JUS maintain records demonstrating due attention to these considerations. Chapter 3 discusses the need to integrate gender considerations into legislative drafting. Further strengthening GBA+ capacities among JUS employees can provide an additional quality filter for gender considerations to be duly reflected within draft bills by federal departments. Advancements are already recorded in this regard in 2018. For example government bills c-68 and c-69 incorporated the "*consideration of health, social and economic effects, including with respect to the intersection of sex and gender with other identity factors*" into environmental impact assessments, energy decisions and fishery decisions.

2.2.5. Federal departments

In Canada, as in most OECD countries which implement gender mainstreaming, the main responsibility for gender-based analysis lies within the federal line departments. Federal departments are expected to put in place adequate governance structures for GBA+. These include a formal GBA+ policy statement or intent; a GBA+ responsibility centre that leads, supports, and monitors GBA+ implementation and serves as a point of liaison with the broader Government of Canada GBA+ network; an intra-departmental network or working group dedicated to GBA+; and a senior management representative to champion and lead GBA+. These processes have indeed been proven central for effective gender mainstreaming. Sweden, another OECD country that pioneering the development of gender mainstreaming and budgeting, has put in place a similar governance structure (see Box 2.5) The OECD experience shows that unless such governance elements are in place, the gender mainstreaming initiatives in line departments often stall and do not yield results.

Historically, the implementation of GBA+ across federal departments has been uneven (Office of the Auditor General Canada, 2016[30]). The different barriers that departments are facing in the implementation of GBA+ are described in detail in the 2015 Audit of the Office of the Auditor General (OAG) on implementing GBA+. The barriers identified include the limited capacity for applying gender-based analysis; and absence of quality control and limited assessment of the effectiveness of gender-based analysis practices (Office of the Auditor General Canada, 2016[30]). These findings were echoed in June 2016 by reports from the Standing Committee on the Status of Women, and the Public Accounts Committee of the House of Commons.

Box 2.5. Role of line ministries in gender mainstreaming in Sweden

Every Minister in the Government of Sweden is responsible for gender mainstreaming in his or her areas of responsibility. The Minister for Gender Equality is responsible for coordination, development and follow-ups of the gender mainstreaming work. In addition, the Division of Gender Equality is responsible for managing and coordinating the gender mainstreaming work within the Government Offices. Since 2003, there is a gender mainstreaming coordinator within all line ministries with the Government offices of Sweden. A structured, systematic work with gender mainstreaming is conducted within all line ministries; every line ministry is to develop an Annual Action Plan for gender mainstreaming. This is the responsibility of the co-ordinator for gender mainstreaming at each line ministry. The gender focal point is responsible for coordination and support of gender mainstreaming work in his/her ministry. This person is often also the Budget Officer of the line ministry. The focal point for gender mainstreaming attends meetings of a standing intra-ministerial working group on gender mainstreaming in the Government offices. All ten line ministries and the Prime Minister's Office have a Gender Mainstreaming Coordinator.

Source: Government of Sweden 2018

The early indications show that the strong political commitment to GBA+ seems to have accelerated progress in its implementation, and in the uniformity of its implementation, by federal departments. This progress is also recorded in the findings of the SWC Annual Implementation Surveys in 2016 and 2017. Building on this momentum, and to fully implement GBA+ as a transformational tool, further progress would be beneficial in the following areas:

- Increased access to data by federal agencies at earlier stages of policy discussions would improve policy design and lead to more complete gender assessment. SWC and Statistics Canada are already working together to support departments in boosting data-related capacities. In addition, civil society organisations, research centres and gender equality advocacy groups can be important allies in gathering information about the impact of government policies.

- Departments would also benefit from more sector-specific policy guidance on gender equality objectives. While some federal departments have developed action plans for the implementation of GBA+, a common feature of these action plans is the focus on governance processes regarding *how* to implement GBA+ (e.g., a formal GBA+ policy statement or intent, appointing a senior GBA+ champion), rather than dealing with substantial gender equality objectives or goals. A broad-based departmental consultation on gender equality impacts from the outset of each government's term could support federal departments in identifying the relevance of gender equality aspects in their own areas of responsibility. The value of such a consultative exercise could also be enhanced through making the results publicly available (see Chapter 3). In addition, considering a repository of GBA+ good practices where departments can find sector-specific guidance and inspiration in a timely manner could also boost the effectiveness and impact of gender mainstreaming initiatives (see Chapter 3).

- Finally, investing in departmental capacities to incorporate gender considerations more systematically in strategic planning, data collection and analysis, stakeholder engagement, and evaluation functions would be beneficial for gender mainstreaming efforts to have a transformational impact on policy decisions (see Chapter 3).

2.2.6. Statistics Canada

The critical role and responsibility of statistical agencies in advancing gender equality is underlined in the 2015 Recommendation. Statistics Canada plays an increasingly important role for the government-wide implementation of gender equality goals (e.g. tracking implementation of international commitments under CEDAW). In doing so, Statistics Canada works closely with other federal government departments and agencies, often on a cost-recovery basis, to provide sex-disaggregated data; and support further data development initiatives, notably on social surveys. Statistics Canada also works to build departmental knowledge and capacity on GBA+ through data finding workshops. Most recently, through its Budget 2018, the Government of Canada proposed to invest resources for Statistics Canada to create a new Centre for Gender, Diversity and Inclusion Statistics: "*a centre that will act as GBA+ data hub to support future, evidence-based policy development and decision-making*".

To support the implementation of the government's commitment to gender equality, Statistics Canada is orienting its future work towards supporting departments in the development of progress and impact indicators; and development of a gender portal in collaboration with SWC in the framework of Canada's broader open government efforts. The aim is to provide federal departments and civil society with a “one stop shop” for sex-disaggregated data. These initiatives and increasing support of Statistics Canada to gender equality work is commended. Indeed, the 2015 Recommendation highlights the critical importance of data collecting and producing bodies in providing the decision makers with tools necessary for informed and evidence-based policies, budgets and services.

Moving forward, the OECD sees multiple benefits for Statistics Canada to play an enhanced role in support of impact analysis of gender equality initiatives across different policy fields. The SDGs agenda, with its emphasis upon measurable progress in particular policy areas including gender equality, provides another institutional incentive to engage more fully with data identification and analysis. Statistics Canada is already working on data integration aimed at demonstrating social and economic impacts of policy initiatives (e.g. social determinants of health incomes), and extending this work stream to encompass gender equality impacts would be a strong support for the sustainability of this agenda into the future.

2.3. A whole-of-state aspiration for the governance of gender equality

There is growing recognition across the OECD that horizontal policy goals – such as inclusive growth, sustainable and green development, gender equality and diversity – cannot be implemented in isolation by the executive branch. In respect of constitutional frameworks and beyond accountability functions, the benefits of collaboration across the branches of power, levels of government and with non-governmental stakeholders are articulated in many OECD instruments such as the 2015 Recommendation and 2017 OECD Recommendation on Open Government. The inherently cross-cutting nature of gender equality work goes well beyond the scope of the executive branch. Indeed, all state action from laws and policies to budgets and judicial decisions can either facilitate or hinder progress in gender equality. For example, enhancing gender equality and diversity in the justice system can reduce barriers for women's access to justice, such as stigma associated with reporting violence and abuse. Therefore, in recognition of the constitutional roles and prerogatives and independence of branches of power, Canada is encouraged to develop a collaborative approach across the executive, legislative and judiciary, and levels of government by exploring synergies and sharing examples of what works can accelerate progress in gender equality (see Figure 2.3).

Figure 2.3. A system-wide approach to gender equality

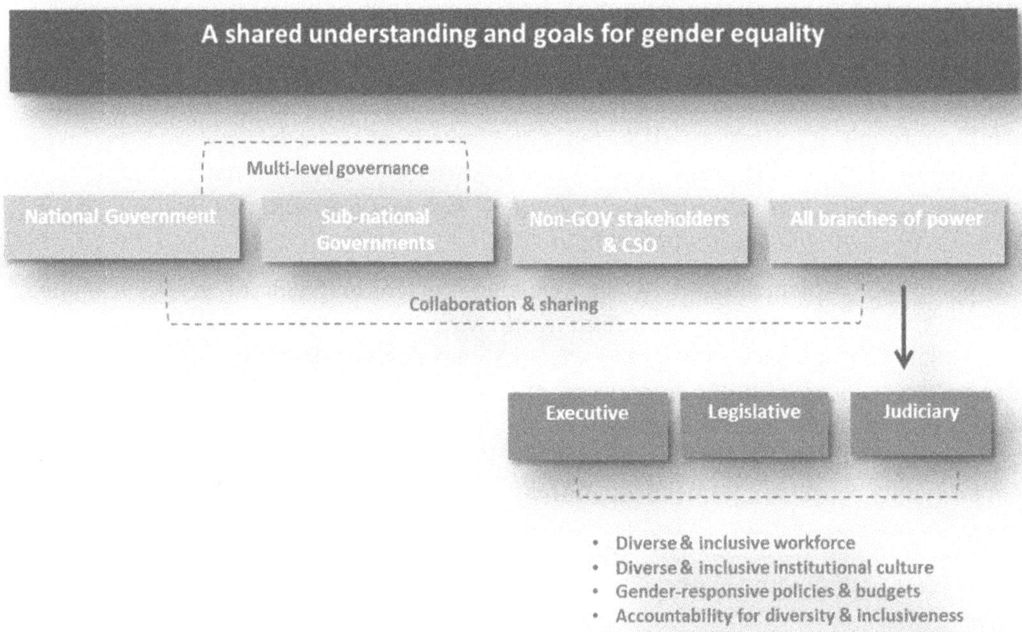

Source: OECD

While cross-branch collaboration is not yet a widespread practice across the OECD, a small but increasing number of governments have put forward such initiatives. Mexico provides an interesting example in the area of gender equality. While Mexico's National Program for Equality of Opportunity and Non-Discrimination Against Women (PROIGUALDAD) mainly addresses the executive branch, it also identifies aspirational goals for the legislature and judiciary, which include goals to promote parity in the allocation of managerial posts in the judicial and legislative branches (OECD, 2017[28]). Similar examples of cross-branch collaboration can be also found for other policy initiatives. For example, within the Open Government Partnership, the President of the Republic of Costa Rica and the Presidents of the three powers of the Republic of Costa Rica (which in Costa Rica are the Executive, the Legislative Assembly and the Supreme Court) and the Supreme Electoral Tribunal signed a joined declaration committing Costa Rica to move towards an open state (OECD, 2016[31]) (see Box 2.6).

The assessment of mechanisms for state-wide collaboration for gender equality in Canada is beyond the scope of this Review. Preliminary indications suggest however the absence of a systematic approach for such collaboration across the branches of power beyond regular accountability functions. The results of the 2016 OECD Surveys on Gender-sensitive Practices in the Legislative and Judiciary have also shown that neither the Canadian legislative branch nor the Canadian judiciary at the federal level has adopted framework strategies or policies that govern gender equality within their areas of authority. Moving forward, Canada can consider kicking-off a cross-branch conversation about how the country can best exploit synergies in advancing shared gender equality goals. As a first step, roundtables or expert meetings could provide useful platforms in this regard.

Box 2.6. Example of cross-branch collaboration for horizontal initiatives

The Declaration for the Creation of an Open State in Costa Rica

On 25 November 2015 the President of the Republic and the Presidents of the three powers of the Republic of Costa Rica (which in Costa Rica are the Executive, the Legislative Assembly and the Supreme Court) and the Supreme Electoral Tribunal signed a joined declaration committing Costa Rica to move towards an open state. The declaration states that each branch will build a plan of priority actions to "promote a policy of openness, transparency, accountability, participation and innovation in favour of the citizens", which will be included in the institutional strategic plans and will be evaluated annually. The powers also agreed to strengthen and develop the mechanisms of citizen participation in order to contribute to a closer relationship between civil society and the leaders and to provide access to public information through the use of new technologies. Costa Rica is the only country in the world to have signed such a promising declaration bringing together all the powers of the state. The declaration has significant potential to guide the country's future open state agenda. In order for it not to remain on paper, the country will now need to underpin its good will with concrete actions. This includes involving the subnational and local governments, decentralized public institutions, independent state institutions, the business sector, media, academia and civil society to join forces to build an open state in Costa Rica.

Sources: (OECD, 2016[32])

2.4. Federal, Provincial and Territorial (FPT) collaboration

The Canadian Constitution defines the exclusive powers of federal parliament and provincial legislatures. In Canada, while provinces exercise constitutional powers in their own right, territories exercise delegated powers under the authority of the Parliament of Canada. Provincial and territorial governments are in charge of gender equality policies under their jurisdictions. The main coordination mechanism addressing national gender equality issues is the forum of FPT Ministers Responsible for the Status of Women. The FPT Ministers meet annually to share information, exchange best practices and explore issues that affect Canadian women and girls including violence against women and girls, women's economic security, and women in leadership.

While this Ministerial coordination mechanism is a positive initiative, its effectiveness could be maximised with a pan-Canadian gender equality framework, addressing international commitments under CEDAW, the SDGs and the 2015 Recommendation (see Chapter 1). Such a framework would allow gender equality discussions can become easier to frame; and collective progress could become easier to measure. Similar concerns were raised by the CEDAW Committee who recommended that Canada *strengthen the implementation of gender equality policies at the provincial and territorial levels and ensure that all government bodies involved receive sustained guidance and support in their implementation efforts.* (United Nations, 2016[21]).

In addition, while the outcomes of annual FPT meetings are communicated through news releases, communication remains somewhat fragmented. There is no single platform where Canadians can easily track the outcomes of annual discussions and track progress over time. Such a platform could significantly raise the profile and visibility of the FPT forum and further improve its effectiveness by making progress easier to monitor.

Beyond co-ordination structures, other OECD countries with federal and quasi-federal government structures are taking innovative approaches to implementation of gender equality on a nationwide basis. An interesting example comes from Mexico where INMUJERES – the federal gender equality institution – launched an online platform showing the performance of 32 states in relation to gender equality. This highlights good practices and fosters peer pressure among states to advance gender equality outcomes (see Box 2.7). Similar developments in Canada may also help advance nation-wide progress.

Box 2.7. Cross-state collaboration on gender equality in Mexico

The Instancias de las Mujeres en las Entidades Federativas (IMEFs) are state-level women's institutes in Mexico that have come into being over the past decade to co-ordinate and drive gender-equality policy. Yet, from one state to another their legal status and institutional standing varies – from ministerial status to decentralised body, general directorate and autonomous body. Mexico's federal system precludes IMEFs from any formal ties with INMUJERES - a federal institution which has no authority over them. INMUJERES therefore uses collaborative agreements with state governments and IMEFs to channel federal funds into gender equality programmes at the state level. For almost a decade, INMUJERES has lent financial and technical support to the IMEFs and their municipal counterparts (IMMs) as part of the Programme for Strengthening Gender Mainstreaming. However, in many instances the direct financial aid that INMUJERES awarded was not enough in itself to set the gender apparatus in motion at sub-national levels. In 2016, INMUJERES (with UN Women) launched an online platform, "México rumbo a la igualdad" (Mexico on the way to equality). Its aim is to showcase the progress made by 32 states in gender mainstreaming in public policies, state budgets and public accounts. The tool seeks to help states track their progress against each other and identify specific action that they need to take – e.g. harmonise laws and policies.

Source: (OECD, 2017[28])

References

Andalusian Regional Government Administration (2014), *PROGRESS IN THE ANDALUSIAN GRB INITIATIVE: GENDER AUDITS*, https://www.wu.ac.at/fileadmin/wu/d/i/vw3/Session_3_Cirujano_Gualda_Romero.pdf (accessed on 17 May 2018). [54]

Australian Government((n.d.)), *National Women's Alliances | Department of the Prime Minister and Cabinet*, 2018, https://www.pmc.gov.au/office-women/grants-and-funding/national-womens-alliances (accessed on 17 May 2018). [48]

Batliwala, S., S. Rosenhek and J. Miller (2013), "WOMEN MOVING MOUNTAINS: COLLECTIVE IMPACT OF THE DUTCH MDG3 FUND HOW RESOURCES ADVANCE WOMEN'S RIGHTS AND GENDER EQUALITY", https://www.awid.org/sites/default/files/atoms/files/Women%20Moving%20Mountains.pdf. [46]

Bochel, H. and A. Berthier (2018), *SPICe Briefing: Committee witnesses: gender and representation*, https://sp-bpr-en-prod-cdnep.azureedge.net/published/2018/2/27/Committee-witnesses--gender-and-representation/SB%2018-16.pdf (accessed on 17 May 2018). [52]

Bohnet, I. (2016), *What works: Gender Equality by Design*, Harvard University Press. [16]

Canadian Feminist Alliance for International Action (FAFIA) (2016), *Because its 2016! A National Gender Equality Plan*, http://tbinternet.ohchr.org/Treaties/CEDAW/Shared%20Documents/CAN/INT_CEDAW_NGO_CAN_25417_E.pdf (accessed on 12 December 2017). [23]

Canadian Institute for Advanced Research & Vancouver School of Economics (2016), *Earnings Inequality and the Gender Pay Gap*, http://faculty.arts.ubc.ca/nfortin/Fortin_EarningsInequalityGenderPayGap.pdf. [6]

Catalyst (2017), *Women In Male-Dominated Industries And Occupations*, http://www.catalyst.org/knowledge/women-male-dominated-industries-and-occupations. [10]

Congressional Budget Office (2016), *CBO's 2016 Long-Term Projections for Social Security: Additional Information*, https://www.cbo.gov/sites/default/files/114th-congress-2015-2016/reports/52298-socialsecuritychartbook.pdf. [62]

Downes, R., L. Von Trapp and S. Nicol (2016), "Gender budgeting in OECD countries", *OECD Journal on Budgeting* 3, http://www.oecd.org/gender/Gender-Budgeting-in-OECD-countries.pdf. [59]

EIGE (2018), *Spain – Structures*, http://eige.europa.eu/gender-mainstreaming/countries/spain/structures. [27]

European Parliament (2016), *Report on Gender Mainstreaming in the work of the European Parliament - A8-0034/2016*, http://www.europarl.europa.eu/sides/getDoc.do?type=REPORT&reference=A8-2016- [51]

0034&language=EN (accessed on 17 May 2018).

European Parliament (2003), *European Parliament resolution on gender mainstreaming in the European Parliament (2002/2025(INI))*, http://www.europarl.europa.eu/sides/getDoc.do?pubRef=-//EP//TEXT+TA+P5-TA-2003-0098+0+DOC+XML+V0//EN. [50]

Flumian, M. (2016), "What Trudeau's committees tell us about his government | Institute on Governance", *Institute on Governance*, https://iog.ca/research-publications/publications/what-trudeaus-committees-tell-us-about-his-government/ (accessed on 21 January 2018). [29]

Goldin, C. (2014), "A Grand Gender Convergence: Its Last Chapter", *American Economic Review*, Vol. 104/4, pp. 1091-1119. [5]

Government of Canada (2018), *Budget 2018: Equality + Growth, A Strong Middle Class*, https://www.budget.gc.ca/2018/docs/plan/budget-2018-en.pdf. [8]

Government of Canada (2018), *Budget Plan + Growth*, https://financebudget.azurewebsites.net/2018/docs/plan/chap-01-en.html?wbdisable=true. [7]

Government of Canada (2018), *Innovation, Science and Economic Development Canada - Canada.ca*, https://www.canada.ca/en/innovation-science-economic-development.html. [44]

Government of Canada (2018), *Mandate Letter Tracker: Delivering results for Canadians*, https://www.canada.ca/en/privy-council/campaigns/mandate-tracker-results-canadians.html (accessed on 10 February 2018). [33]

Government of Canada (2018), *Policy on Results*, https://www.tbs-sct.gc.ca/pol/doc-eng.aspx?id=31300 (accessed on 17 May 2018). [38]

Government of Canada (2017), *Budget 2017: Building a Strong Middle Class*, https://www.budget.gc.ca/2017/docs/plan/budget-2017-en.pdf. [57]

Government of Canada (2017), *Fact Sheet: It's time to pay attention*, http://www.swc-cfc.gc.ca/violence/strategy-strategie/fs-fi-3-en.html. [45]

Government of Canada (2017), *Multilateral Early Learning and Child Care Framework - Canada.ca*, https://www.canada.ca/en/employment-social-development/programs/early-learning-child-care/reports/2017-multilateral-framework.html (accessed on 11 December 2017). [24]

Government of Canada (2017), *Results and Delivery in Canada: Building on momentum*, http://www.fmi.ca/media/1200856/results_and_delivery_building_momentum_october_2017.pdf. [34]

Government of Canada (2016), *Fall Economic Statement 2016*, https://www.budget.gc.ca/fes-eea/2016/docs/statement-enonce/fes-eea-2016-eng.pdf. [56]

Government of Canada (2016), *Increasing Recruitment of Women into the Canadian Armed Forces*. [17]

Government of Canada((n.d.)), *Charter Statements - Canada's System of Justice*, 2018, http://www.justice.gc.ca/eng/csj-sjc/pl/charter-charte/index.html (accessed on 17 May 2018). [41]

Government of Canada((n.d.)), *Employment Insurance Service Quality Review Report: Making Citizens Central*, 2017, https://www.canada.ca/en/employment-social-development/programs/ei/ei-list/reports/service-quality-review-report.html. [43]

Government of Finland (2016), *Government Action Plan For Gender Equality 2016–2019*, https://julkaisut.valtioneuvosto.fi/bitstream/handle/10024/79305/03_2017_Tasa-arvo-ohjelma_Enkku_kansilla.pdf?sequence=1. [19]

Government of Iceland((n.d.)), *Gender Budgeting*, 2018, https://www.government.is/topics/economic-affairs-and-public-finances/gender-budgeting/ (accessed on 16 May 2018). [60]

Government of Spain (2014), *Plan Estratégico de Igualdad de Oportunidades 2014-2016*, http://www.inmujer.gob.es/actualidad/PEIO/docs/PEIO2014-2016.pdf. [20]

Government of Sweden (2014), *Sweden's follow-up of the Platform for Action from the UN's*, https://www.regeringen.se/contentassets/b2f5cc340526433f8e33df3024d510e3/swedens-follow-up-of-the-platform-for-action-from-the-uns-fourth-world-conference-on-women-in-beijing-1995---covering-the-period-between-20092014. [47]

Government of Sweden (2007), *Moving Ahead: Gender budgeting in Sweden*, http://store1.digitalcity.eu.com/store/clients/release/AAAAGNJH/doc/gender-budgeting-in-sweden_2007.09.29-12.22.48.pdf. [65]

House of Commons Canada (2008), *Committee Report No. 9 - FEWO (39-2) - House of Commons of Canada*, http://www.ourcommons.ca/DocumentViewer/en/39-2/FEWO/report-9/. [53]

House of Commons Canada (2007), *Report of the Standing Committee on the Status of Women: The impacts of funding and program changes at Status of Women Canada*, http://www.ourcommons.ca/Content/Committee/391/FEWO/Reports/RP2876038/feworp18/feworp18-e.pdf (accessed on 23 January 2018). [26]

House of Commons Canada((n.d.)), *FEWO - About*, 2018, https://www.ourcommons.ca/Committees/en/FEWO/About (accessed on 17 May 2018). [49]

IMF (2017), *Gender Budgeting in G7 Countries*, https://www.imf.org/en/Publications/Policy-Papers/Issues/2017/05/12/pp041917gender-budgeting-in-g7-countries. [36]

Mahony, T. (2011), "Women and the Criminal Justice System", *Statistics Canada Catalogue no. 89-503-X*, http://www.statcan.gc.ca/pub/89-503-x/2010001/article/11416-eng.pdf (accessed on 17 May 2018). [11]

McInturff, K. and B. Lambert (2016), *Making Women Count: The Unequal Economics of Women's Work*, | Canadian Centre for Policy Alternatives, OXFAM Canada, https://www.policyalternatives.ca/publications/reports/making-women-count-0 (accessed on 01 January 2018). [13]

McKinsey Global Institute (2017), *The power of parity: Advancing women's equality in Canada*, https://www.mckinsey.com/featured-insights/gender-equality/the-power-of-parity-advancing-womens-equality-in-canada (accessed on 16 May 2018). [2]

Moyser, M. (2017), *Women and Paid Work, Statistics Canada, March, available online at: http://www.statcan.gc.ca/pub/89-503-x/2015001/article/14694-eng.htm.* [4]

OECD (2017), *Behavioural Insights and Public Policy: Lessons from Around the World.*, OECD Publishing. [15]

OECD (2017), *Building an inclusive Mexico : Policies and Good Governance for Gender Equality*, OECD Publishing. [28]

OECD (2017), *Recommendation of the Council on Open Government*, http://www.oecd.org/gov/Recommendation-Open-Government-Approved-Council-141217.pdf. [42]

OECD (2017), *The Pursuit of Gender Equality: An Uphill Battle*, OECD Publishing, Paris, http://dx.doi.org/10.1787/9789264281318-en. [1]

OECD (2016), *Open Government The Global Context and the Way Forward*, OECD Publishing. [32]

OECD (2016), "Open Government: The Global Context and The Way Forward", http://www.oecd-ilibrary.org/docserver/download/4216481e.pdf?expires=1516890637&id=id&accname=ocid84004878&checksum=36020513E75CAF56257B41F9DC2A3AFC (accessed on 25 January 2018). [31]

OECD (2015), "Delivering from the Centre: Strengthening the role of the centre of government in driving priority strategies", https://www.oecd.org/gov/cog-2015-delivering-priority-strategies.pdf (accessed on 21 January 2018). [25]

OECD (Forthcoming), *Budgeting in Austria.* [37]

OECD (Forthcoming), *Budgeting Outlook 2018.* [39]

OECD (Forthcoming), *Budgeting Practices and Procedures Dataset.* [58]

OECD (Forthcoming), *Governance Guidelines for Gender Budgeting.* [64]

OECD (forthcoming) (2018), *OECD Economic Surveys: Canada, OECD Publishing, Paris.* [3]

Office of the Auditor General Canada (2016), *Implementing Gender-Based Analysis*, http://www.oag-bvg.gc.ca/internet/English/parl_oag_201602_01_e_41058.html (accessed on 24 January 2018). [30]

Office of the Auditor General of Canada((n.d.)), *The Environment and Sustainable Development Guide*, 2018, http://www.oag-bvg.gc.ca/internet/English/meth_lp_e_19275.html (accessed on 17 May 2018). [55]

OXFAM Canada (2017), *Feminist Scorecard 2017: Tracking government action to advance women's rights and gender equality*, http://www.oxfam.ca (accessed on 11 December 2017). [22]

Schratzenstaller, M. (2014), *The implementation of gender responsive budgeting in Austria as* [35] *central element of a major budget reform*, https://www.wu.ac.at/fileadmin/wu/d/i/vw3/Session_4_Schratzenstaller.pdf.

Sharp, R. and R. Broomhill (2013), *A Case Study of Gender Responsive Budgeting in Australia*, https://consultations.worldbank.org/Data/hub/files/grb_papers_australia_updf_final.pdf. [63]

Status of Women Canada (2017), *It's Time: Canada's Strategy To Prevent and Address Gender-based Violence*, Government of Canada, http://www.swc-cfc.gc.ca/violence/strategy-strategie/GBV_Fact_sheets_2.pdf (accessed on 01 January 2018). [12]

Status of Women Canada((n.d.)), *The History of GBA+ Domestic and International Milestones*. [14]

Swedish Fiscal Policy Council (2016), *Finanspolitiska rådets rapport 2016*, http://www.finanspolitiskaradet.com/download/18.21a8337f154abc1a5dd28c15/1463487699296/Svensk+finanspolitik+2016.pdf. [61]

The Victorian Government (2018), *Safe and Strong: A Victorian Gender Equality Strategy. Achievements Report Year One*, https://www.vic.gov.au/system/user_files/Documents/women/1801009_Safe_and_strong_first_year_report_summary_10_%C6%92_web.pdf (accessed on 17 May 2018). [18]

UK National Audit Office (2016), *Sustainability in the spending review*, https://www.nao.org.uk/wp-content/uploads/2016/07/Sustainability-in-the-Spending-Review.pdf. [40]

United Nations (2016), "Concluding observations on the combined eighth and ninth periodic reports of Canada*", https://documents-dds-ny.un.org/doc/UNDOC/GEN/N16/402/03/PDF/N1640203.pdf?OpenElement (accessed on 11 December 2017). [21]

Wells, M. (2018), *Closing the Engineering Gender Gap*, https://www.design-engineering.com/features/engineering-gender-gap/. [9]

Chapter 3. Delivering gender equality through government policy

This chapter looks at Gender-Based Analysis Plus (GBA+) and its implementation in Canada and provides recommendations to help maximise its potential as a tool for delivering greater gender equality through government policy. It also considers the extent to which the performance and results framework tracks and facilitates outcomes in relation to gender equality. The Government of Canada has a strong focus on results and has recently instituted a Cabinet Committee on Agenda, Results and Communications (ARC) and, to support it, a Results and Delivery Unit (RDU) at the Privy Council Office. The development of the Gender Results Framework as part of Budget 2018 also represents an important step forward. Further development of this Framework should focus on strengthening its upstream linkages - to specific gender equality targets set out in a gender equality strategy for Canada – and its downstream linkages to departmental results and delivery frameworks.

3.1. Introduction

Government policy is more likely to achieve overarching gender equality goals when decision-making tools, from policies and legislation to budgets, regulations and procurement take full account of the different circumstances, needs and challenges of women and men. GBA+ is the main analytical tool that the Government of Canada uses to assess the different impacts of policies and programmes on women and men. The broader results framework can also play a key role in making explicit the links between programmes and gender equality outcomes.

This chapter assesses GBA+ and its implementation in Canada and provides recommendations to maximise its potential as a tool to help deliver gender equality through all aspects of government policy. It also highlights the performance and results mechanisms of the current government and assesses their role in promoting gender responsive policy making.

3.2. GBA+ as a tool to mainstream gender considerations in policy development

GBA+ acts as a key vehicle for accelerating gender equality results in Canada through encouraging an assessment of how diverse groups of women, men and gender-diverse people may be affected by policies, programs and initiatives (see Box 3.1). Box 3.2 provides examples of GBA+. The government committed to gender mainstreaming all legislation, policies and programmes as part of the framework of the Beijing Platform for Action. GBA was developed as a response to this commitment. Over time, GBA has evolved into a modern tool of policy making, integral to gender mainstreaming in Canada. In 2011, SWC rebranded GBA as GBA+ to factor in diverse identity circumstances, such as race, ethnicity, religion, age, and mental or physical disability. In line with the provisions of the 2015 Recommendation, which aims to address multiple dimensions of discrimination, Canada is among the few OECD countries which put a strong emphasis on intersectional identity factors beyond gender. While there is no legislative underpinning for GBA+, since 2016 it has been mandatory that evidence be provided to demonstrate that GBA+ has been completed for all submissions brought before Cabinet and the Treasury Board.

Box 3.1. Gender-based Analysis Plus (GBA+) in Canada

GBA+ is an analytical tool used to assess how diverse groups of women, men and gender-diverse people may experience policies, programs and initiatives. This means that analysts, researchers, evaluators and decision makers are able to continually improve their work and attain better results for Canadian men and women by being more responsive to their specific needs and circumstances. The "plus" in GBA+ acknowledges that GBA goes beyond biological (sex) and socio-cultural (gender) differences. It examines how sex and gender intersect with other identities such as: race, ethnicity, religion, age and mental or physical disability. There is a broad recognition in Canada that without GBA+, there is a risk of missing or misreading the experiences of a significant portion of the Canadian population and –as a consequence – risk developing policies and initiatives that can inadvertently increase inequalities. It is therefore critical that GBA+ is applied to optimise the impact and effectiveness of all federal initiatives.

SWC plays a leadership role in the government-wide implementation of GBA+.

However, the commitment to GBA+ is a shared responsibility across all departments and agencies.

All federal **departments or agencies** are required to provide evidence that they have taken GBA+ considerations into account and to report relevant findings in their Memoranda to Cabinet and Treasury Board Submission. GBA+ can be used to inform the entire policy process, from research and early investigation through to the development of options and strategies. It should also inform implementing (e.g. MOUs, terms and conditions), monitoring, evaluating and communicating an initiative.

Central agencies (PCO, TBS and FIN) play a challenge-function in relation to the GBA+; provide guidance on incorporating GBA+ into Cabinet documents; and apply GBA+ to their internal work.

Action Plan on Gender-based Analysis (2016-2020)

In 2015, the Auditor General of Canada's Report "Implementing Gender-based Analysis" pointed to the need to do more to fully implement GBA+ as a rigorous practice across government. It recommended that SWC, the PCO and TBS work with all federal departments and agencies to identify the barriers to implementing GBA, and to periodically assess and report on progress. It further recommended that SWC assess the resources it needs to deliver on its GBA+ mandate. Subsequent recommendations were made by the Standing Committee on the Status of Women (FEWO).

As a response, SWC, PCO and TBS developed an Action Plan laying out the steps that will be taken in response to the gaps identified by the Auditor General, building on progress and lessons learned. Some commitments of the Action Plan include:

- Better identifying and analysing barriers to GBA+ implementation;
- Mitigating known barriers by enhancing GBA+ tools, training, and resources;
- Creating new forums for networking and collaboration on GBA+, including among senior leaders;
- Updating guidance for developing Memoranda to Cabinet (MC) and TB submissions to include more specific direction on GBA+ ;
- Strengthening the challenge function of central agencies through training; and
- Developing and implementing a more robust framework to monitor progress on GBA+ capacity and implementation across government, as well as identifying GBA+ informed outcomes and results.

Source: Status of Women Canada, Introduction to GBA+ online training [http://www.swc-cfc.gc.ca/gba-acs/course-cours-2017/eng/modA2/modA2_01_01.html]; Action Plan on Gender-based Analysis (2016-2020) http://www.swc-cfc.gc.ca/gba-acs/plan-action-2016-en.html

3.2.1. Strengths and weaknesses in the existing application of GBA+

Important improvements in the implementation of GBA+ have been recorded in recent years, driven by the findings of the OAG in 2015 that the implementation of GBA+ has been uneven across federal departments. In its assessment, the OAG found little evidence that GBA+ had informed and potentially steered Cabinet decision-making process, and made recommendations to address these gaps (Office of the Auditor General Canada,

2016[30]). Subsequent recommendations were made by the Standing Committee on the Status of Women (FEWO) to advance the implementation of GBA+ The recommendations included: the introduction of a legislative basis for the implementation of GBA+; raising awareness on the impacts of GBA+ at the federal level; annual evaluation of the GBA+ online course; and provision of SWC with the adequate financial and human resources to support the implementation of GBA+.

Following the recommendations of the OAG and FEWO, and building on the high level political commitment to the gender equality and inclusion agenda, the regulatory underpinning of GBA+ has gradually been strengthened in parallel to the introduction of gender budgeting. In 2016, the government made it mandatory that evidence be provided to demonstrate that GBA+ has been considered and completed as necessary for all submissions brought before Cabinet and the Treasury Board. In the same year, GBA+ was integrated into the government's new Policy on Results. In 2017, the Minister of Finance advised departments that all budget proposals needed to be accompanied by a GBA+ assessment. Canada is now one the few OECD countries where gender analysis is mainstreamed within routine Cabinet policy process, in accordance with the 2015 Recommendation. Most notably, the Budget 2018 committed to introduce new GBA+ legislation. Work is also underway to make GBA+ mandatory for regulatory impact analysis. Early indications show that these initiatives have already yielded positive impacts on the GBA+ capacity within federal departments and agencies. In addition, since GBA+ became mandatory, more departments appear to be collecting gender-disaggregated data, and have increasingly put in place departmental governance structures to implement GBA+ (Status of Women Canada, 2018).

Sustaining the current momentum for GBA+ will help overcome the remaining departmental barriers to the implementation of GBA+. According to the results of the SWC annual GBA+ Implementation Survey most departments still do not have a GBA+ action plan, and are yet to develop internal governance structures for implementing GBA+. Most GBA+ training remains focussed on policy analysis with room to improve GBA+ integration in program design, delivery legislation, and other areas such as procurement. There is also scope to boost efforts in monitoring GBA+.

Another area where there is scope to improve the impact of GBA+ is the challenge function exercised by the central agencies (see Chapter 2). At present, GBA+ does not have a legislative basis and derives its relevance from a strong political-level commitment; and in practice, central agencies may be reticent to routinely send back Cabinet proposals to line ministries on the grounds of a missing or incomplete GBA+. The future GBA+ legislation, announced in the Budget 2018, provides a significant opportunity to strengthen the role of central agencies in monitoring the implementation of GBA+. The scope of the announced legislation relates to budgeting and expenditure decisions. A Cabinet directive on GBA+ could further strengthen the challenge function of GBA+ in Cabinet proposals.

Box 3.2. Implementing GBA+ in Immigration, Refugees and Citizenship Canada

Immigration, Refugees and Citizenship Canada (IRCC) is the only federal department that is required to conduct and report to Parliament on GBA+. The Immigration and Refugee Protection Act, which came into force in 2002, includes a legislative requirement to provide gender-based analysis of the impact of the Act in an annual report to Parliament. As such, the Act specifically provides that: *"The Minister must ... table in each House of Parliament a report on the operation of this Act in the preceding calendar year"* and *"the report shall include a description of ... a gender-based analysis of the impact of this Act."* The IRCC has a GBA+ unit in the Strategic Policy and Planning Branch, which acts as the functional authority responsible for the department's GBA+ policy and organisational capacity, and a GBA+ Champion who highlights the effectiveness of applying this analysis.

An example of how GBA+ improved decision-making

IRCC applied GBA+ to a sponsorship regulation. In 2016, as part of a Ministerial mandate commitment, IRCC developed a proposal to remove a regulatory requirement for sponsored spouses and partners of Canadian citizens and permanent residents to live with their sponsor for two years as a condition to maintaining their permanent resident status.

The analysis recognised that a sponsored spouse or partner can be vulnerable for many reasons, including gender, age, official language proficiency, isolation and financial dependence, and that these factors can create an imbalance between the sponsor and their spouse or partner. It was further assessed that the conditional permanent residence two-year co-habitation requirement could compound these vulnerabilities in situations of domestic abuse. Noting that women made up a majority (70%) of affected individuals who submitted requests to IRCC for an exception to the condition on the basis of abuse or neglect, IRCC assessed that this regulatory requirement may potentially result in vulnerable spouses and partners remaining in abusive relationships out of fear of losing their permanent resident status in Canada.

The conditional permanent residence requirement was repealed on April 18, 2017.

3.2.2. Linkages between GBA+ and Cabinet processes

GBA+ is fully integrated within the routine Cabinet policy process, and this appears to have improved the extent and quality of this policy assessment tool. These requirements have brought about a cultural change in departments whereby GBA+ is being taken more seriously. Moving forward, its sustainability and impact can be underpinned by the federal administration's willingness and ability to fully integrate the gender analysis within the results and delivery agenda.

Although there are benefits to linking GBA+ with Cabinet policy processes, a number of factors are relevant in assessing the effectiveness of the tool:

1. Firstly, the principle of Cabinet confidentiality can place informal constraints on the ability of SWC to support departments directly in the preparation of Cabinet submissions. The principle can also make it difficult for the parliament and civil society to scrutinise the quality and rigour of gender analysis.
2. Secondly, the Cabinet submissions are generally prepared under tight timelines. This can make it difficult for policy makers to undertake a meaningful gender analysis, especially when the data and knowledge about gender equality needs in a given sector may not be readily available. For GBA+ to have maximum usefulness, it needs to be factored in to the earliest stages of policy making, and this is not yet the uniform practice in Canada.
3. Thirdly, GBA+ has been long perceived by the federal departments as a narrow tool, a check list, which is closely linked to discrete processes such as the preparation of Cabinet and budget proposals and Treasury Board submissions. A culture change is required to reposition GBA+ as a broader and more comprehensive instrument that can be applied to multiple government activities on an ongoing basis.

One way of boosting the impact of GBA+ on policy decisions is through careful but systematic application of the principle of transparency in respect of GBA+ analysis, in a manner that is respectful of Canada's robust principle of Cabinet confidentiality (see Chapter 4). The instigation of broad-based stakeholder consultation at the beginning of each government term to identify general and sector-specific priorities for gender equality is another potential way forward (also see Chapter 4 on citizen consultation). There is also scope to further embed GBA+ across the different phases of the policy cycle, from problem definition to evaluation and impact analysis. The recently announced commitment to enact GBA+ is likely to help encourage this, alongside efforts by SWC to raise departmental awareness in this area.

3.3. Integrating a gender dimension into the results and delivery approach

3.3.1. The results and delivery approach

The government of Canada has outlined its commitment to evidence-based decision making and to delivering real and meaningful results for Canadians. The importance of this political commitment is underlined by the establishment of a Cabinet Committee on Agenda, Results and Communications (ARC) and, to support it, a Results and Delivery Unit (RDU) at the PCO[1] (see Box 3.3). The President of the Treasury Board of Canada has also been given a mandate to ensure departments use the best available information, measure the impact of their programmes and improve parliamentary reporting.

3.3.2. Setting overarching government priorities

The government sets out its high level commitments in individual mandate letters, addressed from the Prime Minister to each minister, outlining overall expectations as well as more specific policy objectives. Consistent with the government's emphasis upon the principles of open and transparent government (see Section 4.2), these documents were made public for the first time in 2016. In total there are 30 mandate letters containing, as of October 2017, 406 commitments (Government of Canada, 2018[33])

Box 3.3. New elements of the federal strategic planning framework

The Committee on Agenda, Results and Communications

In November 2015, the Government created a new Cabinet Committee on Agenda, Results and Communications (ARC), chaired by the Prime Minister and tasked with setting the government's forward agenda, tracking progress on priorities, and considering strategic communications.

Results and Delivery Unit

In January 2016, a new Results and Delivery Unit (RDU), housed in the PCO, was established to support the ARC, the Prime Minister and federal departments. It has 15 staff and its purpose is to track departmental performance and report to Cabinet Ministers and the Prime Minister on potential obstacles, or opportunities, that might affect key platform promises. The new unit also supports efforts to monitor delivery and address implementation obstacles, and facilitates the work of government by developing tools, guidance and learning activities on implementing an outcome-focused approach.

The mandate letters direct each minister to track and regularly report on progress against their commitments, assess the effectiveness of ongoing work, and invest resources to achieve results for Canadians on things that matter. Progress against delivering these commitments is highlighted in an online Mandate Letter Tracker[2]. This platform helps Canadians hold the government accountable for delivering high level commitments and, in many respects, represents advanced international practice. Commitments are aligned under one of 12 overarching priorities for government – see Figure 3.1– which are for the most part drawn from the policy-framing Speech from the Throne.

Figure 3.1. Online Mandate Letter Tracker

Source: (Government of Canada, 2018[33])

At present there is no formal link between the 12 overarching priorities and Deputy-Minister level committees (also referred to as Deputy-Minister Taskforces). These committees are generally aimed at longer-term reflection. However, there is a significant degree of alignment between these priorities and committee mandates, and related topics may be brought to Deputy Minister Committees at the discretion of the Chair. In addition, the Prime Minister has identified himself as the lead on the "Diverse and Inclusive Canada" priority and has set up a working group to deliver in this area.

Each priority has a Results and Delivery Charter, setting out a plan for delivery and a reporting framework to enable progress to be tracked. Departments set out the intended outcome and (short, medium and long term) key indicators that support its achievement. Outcomes may be cross-cutting, to help leverage joint-working between departments.

Work is ongoing to align these indicators with those of ongoing departmental results frameworks, to the extent appropriate. The existing disparity of approach can mean that departments are not yet routinely collecting the information required to report against overarching government priorities through their existing business processes (see below). Indeed, the RDU has already come up against challenges in collating information from departments for this task. In some cases over the longer term it is likely that new data, more specifically linked to the priorities, will have to be collected by departments as part of a more organised data strategy.

3.3.3. Departmental performance reporting

In 1997, Canada split its Departmental Expenditure Plans into Reports on Plans and Priorities and Departmental Performance Reports. These tools, now called Departmental Plans and Departmental Results Reports, continue to form the foundation of Canada's current departmental monitoring structure.

Departmental Plans (DPs) are forward-looking documents that describe departmental priorities, expected results and associated resource requirements covering three fiscal years. Where the department is a chartered department, the priorities set out in the DP should show alignment with the Results and Delivery Charter. To ensure that departments have data to support the proposed indicators, they must also present a plan of how they will obtain the data to track progress.

By contrast, Departmental Results Reports (DRRs) are an account of actual performance for the most recently completed fiscal year, reporting against the plans, priorities and expected results set out in their respective DPs.

The Policy on Results, introduced in 2016[3], sets out the Departmental Results Framework for how departments achieve and report results. As part of this, departments must collect key performance information on each programme in Performance Information Profiles (PIPs). The Policy on Results provides guidance on how departments can use their performance information to support funding requests. The Directive on Results (2016) outlines requirements for supporting the implementation of the Policy on Results, including the identification of roles and responsibilities for Canadian federal departmental officials.

Role of the Treasury Board Secretariat (TBS)[4]

The Treasury Board is a senior committee of Cabinet that functions as the government's management board and, supported by its Secretariat, it oversees the operations of the entire federal government. One of the key areas where it performs this oversight role is in relation to performance management. TBS reviews DPs and DRRs and makes sure they conform to their central guidance. The RDU at PCO also now plays a guiding role in relation to performance reporting, to ensure that it is aligned with overarching government priorities.

A summary of the overall results and delivery system is provided in Figure 3.2, with the key elements explained in Box 3.4.

Figure 3.2. Federal government results and delivery system

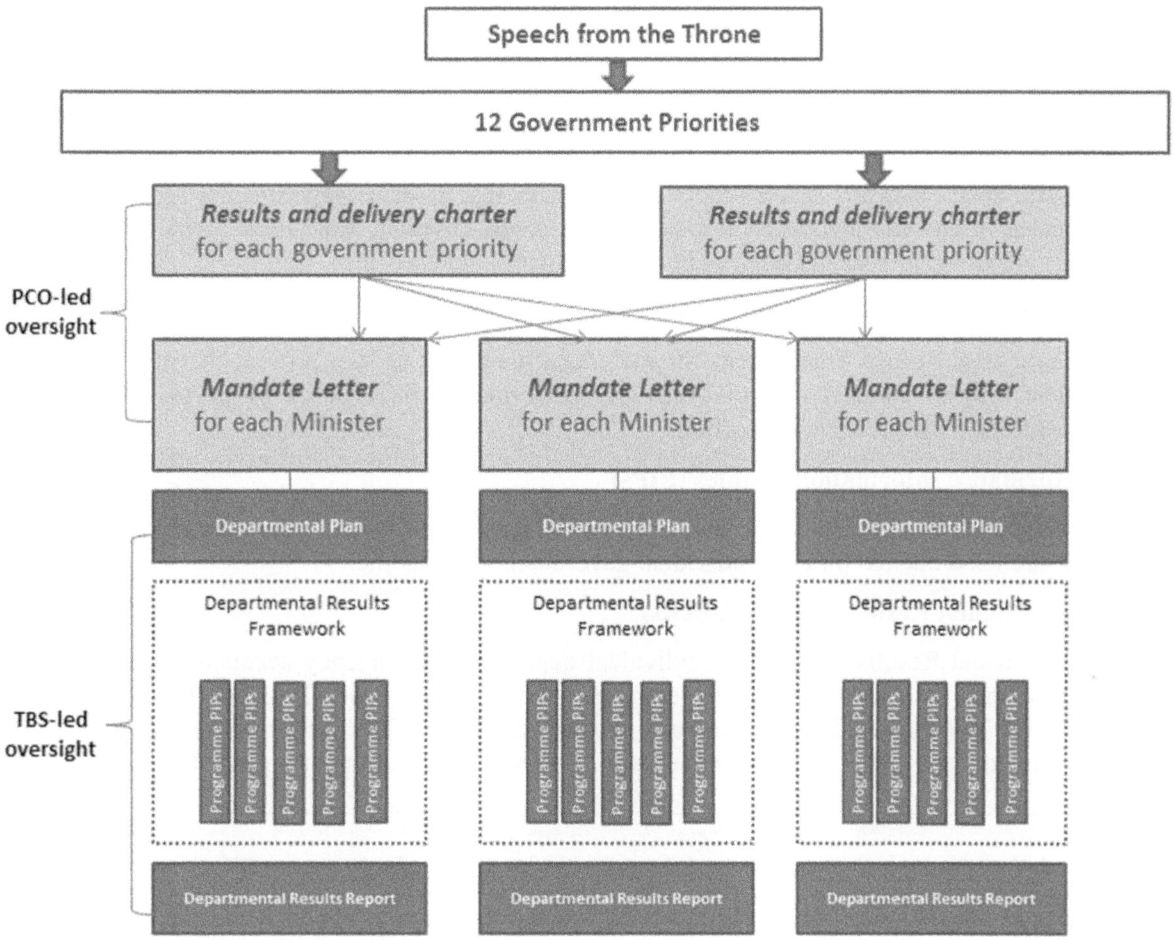

Source: OECD, adapted from (Government of Canada, 2017[34])

Box 3.4. Elements of the results and delivery system in Canada's federal government

Results and Delivery Charter

This is a new Cabinet document that is used as the basis for reporting progress against the 12 overarching priorities for government. For each priority area, departments set out the intended outcome and key indicators that support it.

Mandate Letters

Mandate letters, from the Prime Minister to each minister, outline overall expectations as well as more specific policy objectives for respective ministers. These letters highlight how all ministers can make a contribution to government-wide commitments.

Departmental Plans (DPs)

Departmental Plans are forward-looking documents that describe departmental priorities, expected results and associated resource requirements covering three fiscal years. These Plans are tabled in Parliament on or before March 31.

Departmental Results Framework (DRF)

Departmental Results Frameworks for each department and agency provide the structure against which financial and non-financial performance information is provided for estimates and parliamentary reporting.

Performance Information Profiles (PIPs)

Performance Information Profiles contain the key performance information that is measured and tracked for each individual government programme.

Departmental Results Reports (DRRs)

Departmental Results Reports are individual department and agency accounts of actual performance for the most recently completed fiscal year, reported against the plans, priorities and expected results set out in their respective DPs. These reports inform parliamentarians and Canadians of the results achieved by government organisations.

3.3.4. Integrating a gender lens into the results and delivery approach

Canada is already working to strengthen the linkages between its gender assessment tools and the results and delivery framework. The government's high-level commitment to gender equality is embedded in one of the twelve overarching priorities, which provides for a "Diverse and Inclusive Canada". In total, 14 commitments relating to gender sit under this priority and are included in the mandate letters to various ministers. 11 of these commitments are included in the mandate letter for the Minister of Status of Women, three are included in the mandate letter for the Minister of Employment, Workforce Development and Labour and five appear in the mandate letters of other ministers[5].

SWC are currently developing a standardised framework of indicators for gender equality. This body of indicators will be available for use in populating charters, Departmental Results Frameworks and Performance Information Profiles (see also Chapter 1 on federal gender equality policy).

In terms of including a gender perspective in departmental performance reporting, the Directive on Results includes a number of considerations in relation to gender. Specifically, it requires that departments:

- Consider gender-based analysis in developing their plans for performance measurement at the programme level; and
- Provide descriptive tags for programmes that identify when they impact target groups, such as women.

TBS, as part of its "challenge" function in assessing draft departmental plans and departmental results reports, encourages the integration of gender considerations where appropriate. In addition, all Departmental Plans in 2017-18 include a mandatory GBA+ supplementary information table. SWC works with TBS and departments to support this work and ensure alignment with the indicators framework that it is developing (see also Chapter 2).

TBS has also recently issued guidance to departments on the need to include PIPs for each programme. PIPs identify the performance information for each programme and must build in gender-based analysis where relevant.

Arising from these recent initiatives, many of the tools are in place or are being developed to help departments to integrate gender analysis within their frameworks for results targeting and reporting. It remains early to assess the success of departments in employing these tools, and on delivering impactful, gender-responsive policies. A continued central guidance and oversight role will be important, particularly in helping departments to manage the institutional adaptations and mind-set changes that may be required, if the new approach is to be implemented in a uniform manner (see Chapter 2 for a more detailed assessment of institutional roles and responsibilities).

3.3.5. Enhancing the integration of gender into results and delivery

The results and delivery framework is an important and useful tool which the government can use to deliver more gender equal policymaking. The statement that a "Diverse and Inclusive Canada" is an overarching priority of government provides political momentum that is transmitted across the public administration. In principle this, combined with the new guidance in relation to incorporating gender considerations into departmental performance reporting, should be effective in ensuring integration of gender into the results and delivery approach over time. In practice, however, the Diversity and Inclusion Charter has a narrow focus and does not provide comprehensive guidance for gender equality and diversity policy (see Chapter 2). This leaves the gender approach heavily reliant on political direction. One stakeholder summed up the risks of this approach by observing that "two years of progress could be lost in two minutes" if gender equality were to lose its political support.

The introduction of an overarching framework for gender equality with key indicators is important to provide the foundations for a more sustainable approach to delivering gender equality results. The development of the Gender Results Framework as part of Budget 2018 represents an important step forward in this respect. Further development of this Framework should focus on strengthening its upstream linkages - to specific gender equality targets set out in a gender equality strategy for Canada (see Chapter 1) – and its downstream linkages to departmental results and delivery frameworks. Austria provides a leading international example in this respect (see Box 3.5). Observations in Austria point to this approach securing increased attention for gender equality inside the public administration as well as outside among target groups/stakeholders (Schratzenstaller, 2014[35]). It was also found that "Overall, increased transparency, awareness, and accountability for gender equality issues and objectives, and a richer discussion on gender equality and gender budgeting has been achieved" (IMF, 2017[36]).

Box 3.5. The integration of gender into the performance framework in Austria

Austria's distinctive system of gender budgeting is well integrated within the performance budgeting framework. According to the Federal Budget Law 2013, the outcome objectives specified for each Budget Chapter must include at least one objective related to gender equality; and in turn, each of the "global budgets" and "detailed budgets" must include at least one gender-related output target. In this way, each line ministry is obliged to consider how its activities relate to gender equality, and to design objectives and indicators to promote gender equality in the context of the budget. Moreover, gender equality is one of the dimensions of analysis that must routinely be included in Impact Assessments of new policies. Reporting on the gender-related objectives is covered in the Performance Reports prepared by the Federal Chancellery.

Taken as a whole, therefore, the Austrian system of policy-making is designed to (a) require all ministries to consider gender equality both in their high-level goal-setting and in more detailed specification of outputs and objectives, (b) assess impacts on gender equality in the design of policies, using a standardised assessment template, and apply this assessment both ex ante and ex post, and (c) account for their achievements in gender equality goals and objectives via the annual performance reports.

For a single overview of how ministries are achieving their gender-related objectives, it is necessary to look to the performance reports prepared by the Federal Chancellery. The October "Annual Report on Budget Orientation" not only collates the individual reports from line ministries, but also reconfigures them in order to present a single Gender Statement.

Source: (OECD, Forthcoming[37])

3.4. Evaluation

3.4.1. Background

Canada has long used evaluation to support evidence-based policy development. For over 40 years, evaluation in various forms has been used to assess the performance of programmes operated by government departments. The 2006 Federal Accountability Act introduced a requirement that all grant and contribution programmes be evaluated every five years. The Policy on Results came into effect in 2016 and sets out that departments should have a five-year, rolling departmental evaluation plan (Government of Canada, 2018[38]).

Evaluation Units in each department undertake evaluation studies, but also have a broader role in relation to preparing evaluation planning reports and assessments, developing results-based management accountability frameworks and providing advice and training to programme managers on evaluation. Evaluations can also be conducted by contractors in whole, or in part, particularly when specific technical or subject matter expertise is required. Department managers use evaluation findings and recommendations to support policy and programme improvement, expenditure management, Cabinet decision making, and public reporting.

The TBS Results Division is the technical support unit for evaluations, setting standards, providing central leadership, guidance and support and using evaluation results, where appropriate, in decision making at the centre of government.

3.4.2. Integration of a gender perspective into evaluation

Many of the analytical underpinnings of GBA+ are common to the evaluation procedure: e.g. clarity of policy objectives; interrogation of data sets; questioning of assumptions underlying policy design; and assessment of alternative policy approaches. Indeed, progress in developing system-wide capacity to undertake GBA+ should be expected to have positive spill over effects for capacity to undertake evaluative, evidence-based policy making more generally.

The GBA+ agenda could still, however, be strengthened through more explicit linkages or synergies with the general evaluation framework. This might include the development of specific guidance that requires evaluation units to either systematically take gender into account when evaluating policies and programmes and designing logic frameworks for policies and programmes, or to prioritise evaluations based on the extent to which they are gender focussed. At present, the Directive on Results sets out that, in planning specific evaluations (e.g., in developing the scope and methodology), departments consider issues such as gender where appropriate. In practice, the analytical specialists who undertake policy evaluation generally work on a separate track from the policy designers who are tasked with undertaking GBA+.

3.4.3. Enhancing the integration of gender equality into evaluation

As highlighted by recent research in the OECD, results frameworks, evaluation frameworks (both *ex ante* and *ex post*), programme monitoring systems and other analytical approaches should not be regarded as standalone tools, but as part of the continuum of evaluative information that should be drawn upon by policy makers in the conception, design, planning, monitoring and review of programmes (OECD, Forthcoming[39]). By their nature these evaluative tools can span different time horizons, yield different types of data, deal with different policy domains (e.g. spending versus regulation) and may have different provenance: the task of policy makers is to understand and make use of this data continuum for the purposes of evidence-based policy making and policy review. This work also underlines that evaluation function should be very closely connected with the policy and programme design stage, in developing the necessary logical frameworks and accompanying indicators and data collection strategies to track the implementation and impact of policy choices, including on women and men.

GBA+ is an important addition to this ecology of evaluative instruments, and the results and insights from this tool should be available also to the evaluation community. Where the GBA+ relating to a policy or programme has been well-implemented at the performance measurement strategy stage (e.g. when the program is being set up or renewed), the application of a gender lens to the evaluation can be relatively routine. However, where gender considerations have not been built into a policy or programme's original objectives, a gender lens is not easily applied to its evaluation. As departmental GBA+ and related reporting improves, a gender lens will be automatically built into the evaluation process. Steps are already being taken forward in this area by SWC in collaboration with evaluation managers. TBS has an important supporting role to play in this area. Looking ahead, in ensuring the effectiveness and impact of this initiative it will be important to track the results of such evaluation against specific gender equality targets set out in a gender equality strategy for Canada (see Chapter 1).

3.5. Spending reviews

3.5.1. Background

Since the early 1990s, Canada's experience with spending reviews has taken a number of different approaches, driven by both fiscal imperatives and the objective of better management of public funds and improved outcomes.

Most recently, Canada's current approach to spending review, announced in the 2016 Federal Budget, includes an ongoing commitment to eliminate poorly targeted and inefficient programs, wasteful spending, and ineffective and obsolete government initiatives. The Government began by announcing annual reductions of $221 million (CDN) in professional services, travel and government advertising, and the intent to look at ways to better align government spending with priorities. In line with this commitment, Canada launched four comprehensive departmental reviews in 2016 to ensure ongoing efficiency, effectiveness and value for money. Through Budget 2017, Canada announced three additional departmental reviews, and expanded its review approach to include horizontal reviews, including one covering Business Innovation and Clean Technology, and a second on Federal Real Property.

A departmental spending review may be initiated through a budget announcement or engagement by the President of the Treasury Board with the responsible Minister of the review department. TBS oversees the reviews and provides guidance, but it is typically the review department that is responsible for undertaking the review. Reviews typically take six to twelve months to complete, and culminate in the review Minister's presentation to the Treasury Board. Following Treasury Board consideration of the review results, the President of the Treasury Board provides final recommendations to the Minister of Finance and the Prime Minister to inform budget and Cabinet decisions.

A horizontal spending review is initiated through a budget announcement, and focuses on a specific policy or program area that is of particular interest to the government. Horizontal reviews are led by the President of the Treasury Board, and are carried out by TBS officials working closely with impacted departments. As the responsible Minister, the President of the Treasury Board reports the review results to the Treasury Board, after which final recommendations are made to the Minister of Finance and the Prime Minister to inform future budget and Cabinet decisions.

3.5.2. Integrating a gender perspective into spending reviews

In the past, gender assessment was not routinely included as a dimension of spending review; but in keeping with the guidance on submissions to the Treasury Board, since 2017-18, gender considerations must be presented alongside spending review results in a mandatory GBA+ Appendix. As in the case of GBA+ more generally, improved transparency with regard to the content and nature of the gender analysis, and the mechanisms by which the assessments feed through to spending review decision-making at the Treasury Board, would help to underpin public trust in the quality and impact of this dimension of the spending review process.

The overall gender impact of a spending review exercise has also been assessed in the past by the Treasury Board when it undertook an analysis of the decisions as part of the Deficit Reduction Action Plan in 2012. However, this assessment was undertaken at the end of the spending review. Earlier timing of this assessment would ensure that it can feed into the decision-making process.

3.5.3. Enhancing the integration of gender into spending reviews

It is important that the gender-based analysis accompanying spending review submissions to Treasury Board are of a high standard. One way to spur increased focus in this area would be for the TBS to underline the importance of information from the GBA+ Appendix to the Treasury Board assessment of departmental submissions. Further, TBS could use the information provided by departments as a basis for further analysis to inform decision-making by the Treasury Board. This may involve providing an assessment of different spending review packages and how they would impact gender equality – building on the priorities of the proposed federal gender equality strategy - as part of the decision-making process. It would be similar to how, for example, the UK Government considers the impact of spending review on environmental sustainability (see Box 3.6). In parallel, if gender considerations were more explicitly embedded into the programme and policy design cycle, including evaluation frameworks, the results of these gender-sensitive evaluations of programme and policy performance could also support spending review decisions.

Box 3.6. How the UK 2015 Spending Review took account of environmental issues

The UK Government has a wide range of environmental and sustainable development objectives. The 2015 spending review was an important opportunity for HM Treasury to encourage a coordinated approach to meeting environmental targets. The design of the spending review gave departments the scope to put forward information on environmental risks, impacts and obligations as part of their bids and HM Treasury took steps to encourage departments to do so. HM Treasury asked departments to provide a summary of the impact of their bids on carbon targets and advised their teams facing spending departments to consider climate change, energy, fuel poverty and air quality legislation while assessing departmental bids. As a result, HM Treasury reported that some departments improved the way it made the case for its spend on environment objectives and were better placed to quantify the associated benefits than in previous spending reviews.

HM Treasury took the step of preparing a provisional analysis of the impact of the spending review on environmental objectives. This analysis, undertaken during the spending review, assessed the extent to which collective bids would have a material effect on government's ability to meet objectives.

Source: (UK National Audit Office, 2016[40])

Notes

[1] Central government delivery units such as this are a relatively new phenomenon, first implemented in the UK in 1999, and but now adopted in jurisdictions ranging from Ontario and Maryland to Singapore.

[2] https://www.canada.ca/en/privy-council/campaigns/mandate-tracker-results-canadians.html

[3] This replaces policies including the Policy on Management, Resources and Result Structures and the Policy on Evaluation.

[4] The role of TBS in gender-based analysis is discussed in detail in Chapter 2.

[5] The total does not sum to 14 as for three of the commitments, two or more ministers work together.

References

Andalusian Regional Government Administration (2014), *PROGRESS IN THE ANDALUSIAN GRB INITIATIVE: GENDER AUDITS*, https://www.wu.ac.at/fileadmin/wu/d/i/vw3/Session_3_Cirujano_Gualda_Romero.pdf (accessed on 17 May 2018). [54]

Australian Government((n.d.)), *National Women's Alliances | Department of the Prime Minister and Cabinet*, 2018, https://www.pmc.gov.au/office-women/grants-and-funding/national-womens-alliances (accessed on 17 May 2018). [48]

Batliwala, S., S. Rosenhek and J. Miller (2013), "WOMEN MOVING MOUNTAINS: COLLECTIVE IMPACT OF THE DUTCH MDG3 FUND HOW RESOURCES ADVANCE WOMEN'S RIGHTS AND GENDER EQUALITY", https://www.awid.org/sites/default/files/atoms/files/Women%20Moving%20Mountains.pdf. [46]

Bochel, H. and A. Berthier (2018), *SPICe Briefing: Committee witnesses: gender and representation*, https://sp-bpr-en-prod-cdnep.azureedge.net/published/2018/2/27/Committee-witnesses--gender-and-representation/SB%2018-16.pdf (accessed on 17 May 2018). [52]

Bohnet, I. (2016), *What works: Gender Equality by Design*, Harvard University Press. [16]

Canadian Feminist Alliance for International Action (FAFIA) (2016), *Because its 2016! A National Gender Equality Plan*, http://tbinternet.ohchr.org/Treaties/CEDAW/Shared%20Documents/CAN/INT_CEDAW_NGO_CAN_25417_E.pdf (accessed on 12 December 2017). [23]

Canadian Institute for Advanced Research & Vancouver School of Economics (2016), *Earnings Inequality and the Gender Pay Gap*, http://faculty.arts.ubc.ca/nfortin/Fortin_EarningsInequalityGenderPayGap.pdf. [6]

Catalyst (2017), *Women In Male-Dominated Industries And Occupations*, [10]

http://www.catalyst.org/knowledge/women-male-dominated-industries-and-occupations.

Congressional Budget Office (2016), *CBO's 2016 Long-Term Projections for Social Security: Additional Information*, https://www.cbo.gov/sites/default/files/114th-congress-2015-2016/reports/52298-socialsecuritychartbook.pdf. [62]

Downes, R., L. Von Trapp and S. Nicol (2016), "Gender budgeting in OECD countries", *OECD Journal on Budgeting* 3, http://www.oecd.org/gender/Gender-Budgeting-in-OECD-countries.pdf. [59]

EIGE (2018), *Spain – Structures*, http://eige.europa.eu/gender-mainstreaming/countries/spain/structures. [27]

European Parliament (2016), *Report on Gender Mainstreaming in the work of the European Parliament - A8-0034/2016*, http://www.europarl.europa.eu/sides/getDoc.do?type=REPORT&reference=A8-2016-0034&language=EN (accessed on 17 May 2018). [51]

European Parliament (2003), *European Parliament resolution on gender mainstreaming in the European Parliament (2002/2025(INI))*, http://www.europarl.europa.eu/sides/getDoc.do?pubRef=-//EP//TEXT+TA+P5-TA-2003-0098+0+DOC+XML+V0//EN. [50]

Flumian, M. (2016), "What Trudeau's committees tell us about his government | Institute on Governance", *Institute on Governance*, https://iog.ca/research-publications/publications/what-trudeaus-committees-tell-us-about-his-government/ (accessed on 21 January 2018). [29]

Goldin, C. (2014), "A Grand Gender Convergence: Its Last Chapter", *American Economic Review*, Vol. 104/4, pp. 1091-1119. [5]

Government of Canada (2018), *Budget 2018: Equality + Growth, A Strong Middle Class*, https://www.budget.gc.ca/2018/docs/plan/budget-2018-en.pdf. [8]

Government of Canada (2018), *Budget Plan + Growth*, https://financebudget.azurewebsites.net/2018/docs/plan/chap-01-en.html?wbdisable=true. [7]

Government of Canada (2018), *Innovation, Science and Economic Development Canada - Canada.ca*, https://www.canada.ca/en/innovation-science-economic-development.html. [44]

Government of Canada (2018), *Mandate Letter Tracker: Delivering results for Canadians*, https://www.canada.ca/en/privy-council/campaigns/mandate-tracker-results-canadians.html (accessed on 10 February 2018). [33]

Government of Canada (2018), *Policy on Results*, https://www.tbs-sct.gc.ca/pol/doc-eng.aspx?id=31300 (accessed on 17 May 2018). [38]

Government of Canada (2017), *Budget 2017: Building a Strong Middle Class*, https://www.budget.gc.ca/2017/docs/plan/budget-2017-en.pdf. [57]

Government of Canada (2017), *Fact Sheet: It's time to pay attention*, http://www.swc- [45]

cfc.gc.ca/violence/strategy-strategie/fs-fi-3-en.html.

Government of Canada (2017), *Multilateral Early Learning and Child Care Framework - Canada.ca*, https://www.canada.ca/en/employment-social-development/programs/early-learning-child-care/reports/2017-multilateral-framework.html (accessed on 11 December 2017). [24]

Government of Canada (2017), *Results and Delivery in Canada: Building on momentum*, http://www.fmi.ca/media/1200856/results_and_delivery_building_momentum_october_2017.pdf. [34]

Government of Canada (2016), *Fall Economic Statement 2016*, https://www.budget.gc.ca/fes-eea/2016/docs/statement-enonce/fes-eea-2016-eng.pdf. [56]

Government of Canada (2016), *Increasing Recruitment of Women into the Canadian Armed Forces*. [17]

Government of Canada((n.d.)), *Charter Statements - Canada's System of Justice*, 2018, http://www.justice.gc.ca/eng/csj-sjc/pl/charter-charte/index.html (accessed on 17 May 2018). [41]

Government of Canada((n.d.)), *Employment Insurance Service Quality Review Report: Making Citizens Central*, 2017, https://www.canada.ca/en/employment-social-development/programs/ei/ei-list/reports/service-quality-review-report.html. [43]

Government of Finland (2016), *Government Action Plan For Gender Equality 2016–2019*, https://julkaisut.valtioneuvosto.fi/bitstream/handle/10024/79305/03_2017_Tasa-arvo-ohjelma_Enkku_kansilla.pdf?sequence=1. [19]

Government of Iceland((n.d.)), *Gender Budgeting*, 2018, https://www.government.is/topics/economic-affairs-and-public-finances/gender-budgeting/ (accessed on 16 May 2018). [60]

Government of Spain (2014), *Plan Estratégico de Igualdad de Oportunidades 2014-2016*, http://www.inmujer.gob.es/actualidad/PEIO/docs/PEIO2014-2016.pdf. [20]

Government of Sweden (2014), *Sweden's follow-up of the Platform for Action from the UN's*, https://www.regeringen.se/contentassets/b2f5cc340526433f8e33df3024d510e3/swedens-follow-up-of-the-platform-for-action-from-the-uns-fourth-world-conference-on-women-in-beijing-1995---covering-the-period-between-20092014. [47]

Government of Sweden (2007), *Moving Ahead: Gender budgeting in Sweden*, http://store1.digitalcity.eu.com/store/clients/release/AAAAGNJH/doc/gender-budgeting-in-sweden_2007.09.29-12.22.48.pdf. [65]

House of Commons Canada (2008), *Committee Report No. 9 - FEWO (39-2) - House of Commons of Canada*, http://www.ourcommons.ca/DocumentViewer/en/39-2/FEWO/report-9/. [53]

House of Commons Canada (2007), *Report of the Standing Committee on the Status of Women: The impacts of funding and program changes at Status of Women Canada*, http://www.ourcommons.ca/Content/Committee/391/FEWO/Reports/RP2876038/feworp18/feworp18-e.pdf (accessed on 23 January 2018). [26]

House of Commons Canada((n.d.)), *FEWO - About*, 2018, https://www.ourcommons.ca/Committees/en/FEWO/About (accessed on 17 May 2018). [49]

IMF (2017), *Gender Budgeting in G7 Countries*, https://www.imf.org/en/Publications/Policy-Papers/Issues/2017/05/12/pp041917gender-budgeting-in-g7-countries. [36]

Mahony, T. (2011), "Women and the Criminal Justice System", *Statistics Canada Catalogue no. 89-503-X*, http://www.statcan.gc.ca/pub/89-503-x/2010001/article/11416-eng.pdf (accessed on 17 May 2018). [11]

McInturff, K. and B. Lambert (2016), *Making Women Count: The Unequal Economics of Women's Work*, | Canadian Centre for Policy Alternatives, OXFAM Canada, https://www.policyalternatives.ca/publications/reports/making-women-count-0 (accessed on 01 January 2018). [13]

McKinsey Global Institute (2017), *The power of parity: Advancing women's equality in Canada*, https://www.mckinsey.com/featured-insights/gender-equality/the-power-of-parity-advancing-womens-equality-in-canada (accessed on 16 May 2018). [2]

Moyser, M. (2017), *Women and Paid Work, Statistics Canada, March, available online at: http://www.statcan.gc.ca/pub/89-503-x/2015001/article/14694-eng.htm.* [4]

OECD (2017), *Behavioural Insights and Public Policy: Lessons from Around the World.*, OECD Publishing. [15]

OECD (2017), *Building an inclusive Mexico : Policies and Good Governance for Gender Equality*, OECD Publishing. [28]

OECD (2017), *Recommendation of the Council on Open Government*, http://www.oecd.org/gov/Recommendation-Open-Government-Approved-Council-141217.pdf. [42]

OECD (2017), *The Pursuit of Gender Equality: An Uphill Battle*, OECD Publishing, Paris, http://dx.doi.org/10.1787/9789264281318-en. [1]

OECD (2016), *Open Government The Global Context and the Way Forward*, OECD Publishing. [32]

OECD (2016), "Open Government: The Global Context and The Way Forward", http://www.oecd-ilibrary.org/docserver/download/4216481e.pdf?expires=1516890637&id=id&accname=ocid84004878&checksum=36020513E75CAF56257B41F9DC2A3AFC (accessed on 25 January 2018). [31]

OECD (2015), "Delivering from the Centre: Strengthening the role of the centre of government in driving priority strategies", https://www.oecd.org/gov/cog-2015-delivering-priority-strategies.pdf (accessed on 21 January 2018). [25]

OECD (Forthcoming), *Budgeting in Austria.* [37]

OECD (Forthcoming), *Budgeting Outlook 2018.* [39]

OECD (Forthcoming), *Budgeting Practices and Procedures Dataset.* [58]

OECD (Forthcoming), *Governance Guidelines for Gender Budgeting.* [64]

OECD (forthcoming) (2018), *OECD Economic Surveys: Canada, OECD Publishing, Paris.* [3]

Office of the Auditor General Canada (2016), *Implementing Gender-Based Analysis*, http://www.oag-bvg.gc.ca/internet/English/parl_oag_201602_01_e_41058.html (accessed on 24 January 2018). [30]

Office of the Auditor General of Canada((n.d.)), *The Environment and Sustainable Development Guide*, 2018, http://www.oag-bvg.gc.ca/internet/English/meth_lp_e_19275.html (accessed on 17 May 2018). [55]

OXFAM Canada (2017), *Feminist Scorecard 2017: Tracking government action to advance women's rights and gender equality*, http://www.oxfam.ca (accessed on 11 December 2017). [22]

Schratzenstaller, M. (2014), *The implementation of gender responsive budgeting in Austria as central element of a major budget reform*, https://www.wu.ac.at/fileadmin/wu/d/i/vw3/Session_4_Schratzenstaller.pdf. [35]

Sharp, R. and R. Broomhill (2013), *A Case Study of Gender Responsive Budgeting in Australia*, https://consultations.worldbank.org/Data/hub/files/grb_papers_australia_updf_final.pdf. [63]

Status of Women Canada (2017), *It's Time: Canada's Strategy To Prevent and Address Gender-based Violence*, Government of Canada, http://www.swc-cfc.gc.ca/violence/strategy-strategie/GBV_Fact_sheets_2.pdf (accessed on 01 January 2018). [12]

Status of Women Canada((n.d.)), *The History of GBA+ Domestic and International Milestones.* [14]

Swedish Fiscal Policy Council (2016), *Finanspolitiska rådets rapport 2016*, http://www.finanspolitiskaradet.com/download/18.21a8337f154abc1a5dd28c15/1463487699296/Svensk+finanspolitik+2016.pdf. [61]

The Victorian Government (2018), *Safe and Strong: A Victorian Gender Equality Strategy. Achievements Report Year One*, https://www.vic.gov.au/system/user_files/Documents/women/1801009_Safe_and_strong_first_year_report_summary_10_%C6%92_web.pdf (accessed on 17 May 2018). [18]

UK National Audit Office (2016), *Sustainability in the spending review*, https://www.nao.org.uk/wp-content/uploads/2016/07/Sustainability-in-the-Spending-Review.pdf. [40]

United Nations (2016), "Concluding observations on the combined eighth and ninth periodic reports of Canada*", https://documents-dds-ny.un.org/doc/UNDOC/GEN/N16/402/03/PDF/N1640203.pdf?OpenElement (accessed on 11 December 2017). [21]

Wells, M. (2018), *Closing the Engineering Gender Gap*, https://www.design-engineering.com/features/engineering-gender-gap/. [9]

Chapter 4. Transparency, citizen consultation and accountability

This Chapter looks at the extent to which the Government of Canada is transparent and consultative in its approach to gender equality policy development. A transparent government is critical to building citizen trust and, together with citizen consultation, can underpin evidence-based gender policy-making and improved gender policy results. Canada has taken steps forward in this regard in recent years, and can strengthen this through increased transparency in relation to GBA+ and embedding more systematic and meaningful citizen consultation in the policy development process.

This Chapter also considers scrutiny mechanisms in relation to the government's actions and decisions to achieve greater gender equality. Accountability for the government's actions on gender could be strengthened if the Parliament of Canada and the Canadian Office of the Auditor General build on their successful interventions in the area of GBA+ and incorporate a greater gender perspective in broader aspects of their work.

4.1. Introduction

Openness, transparency and accountability are fundamental to ensuring Canadians' trust in their government. This chapter looks at recent developments in this area and assesses the extent to which openness, transparency and accountability are sufficient to support the delivery of gender equality outcomes.

4.2. Openness and transparency

In the December 2015 Speech from the Throne and the March 2016 Budget, the government committed to raise the bar for openness and transparency. Canada's Open Government Commitments (2016-2018) are structured within four priority areas; open by default; fiscal transparency; innovation, prosperity and sustainable development; and engaging Canadians and the world.

4.2.1. Transparency

Improving the transparency of policy-making processes is a current area of focus for the Government of Canada. As indicated in Section 3.3.2., this commitment is underlined by the online publication, for the first time, of the Mandate Letters from the Prime Minister to all Cabinet ministers. A further example is provided in relation to forthcoming publication of Charter Statements (see Box 4.1). These milestones will ensure that Canadians can better understand the Government's priorities and have the necessary tools to hold government accountable in relation to its commitments[1].

Box 4.1. The Minister of Justice and Charter Statements

The Minister of Justice committed to tabling new "Charter Statements" to accompany proposed bills relating to her area of responsibility. These are prepared to help inform public and parliamentary.

Charter Statements outline some of the key considerations that inform the review of a proposed bill for consistency with the Canadian Charter of Rights and Freedoms. In particular, a Statement identifies Charter rights and freedoms that are potentially engaged by a Bill and provides a brief explanation of the nature of any engagement, in light of the measures being proposed. A Statement may also identify potential justifications for any limits on the rights and freedoms a bill may impose. Gender implications raised by a Bill are included in the Charter Statement.

Furthermore, legislation introduced on June 6, 2017 made the Minister's existing practice a legal duty that extends to all government legislation.

Source: (Government of Canada,(n.d.)$_{[41]}$)

Transparency is particularly relevant in the context of GBA+. New policies go through the Memorandum to Cabinet process for approval, and are routinely subject to GBA+ at multiple stages (as explained in section 3.2). However it is not current practice in Canada for these GBA+ documents to be made available to the public – even after the deliberative phase of policy-making has been completed. This reflects the cautious application of the principle of respect for "Cabinet confidences", which is a keystone of governmental policy-making in Canada as in many other OECD countries.

The absence of proactive disclosure of GBA+ analysis can give rise to a situation where non-governmental stakeholders are unable to form a view on the quality, rigour and relevance of GBA+; nor can they draw upon the findings of high-quality GBA+ work and factor it into their own independent research. In addition, government officials themselves cannot readily access GBA+ related to Cabinet proposals undertaken by other departments, as part of the Cabinet process, which inhibits shared-learning. Addressing this *lacuna* in transparency and open government has the potential to boost the quality and credibility of the GBA+ approach.

The PCO – the authority on matters of Cabinet confidence – notes that the principle of Cabinet confidence applies to policy advices and submissions, and that there is nothing to prevent departments from releasing GBA+ analysis relating to final and announced policies introduced by governments reports (as distinct from the Cabinet memoranda which include advice to government). This could provide factual analysis as well as a short narrative on the impact of GBA+ on the proposal. Indeed, a similar approach is already applied in the case of environmental assessments. The Cabinet Directive on the Environmental Assessment of Policy, Plan and Program Proposals states that when a policy, plan or programme is approved, departments and agencies are tasked with preparing a public statement of environmental impact which are all accessible to the public through the Canadian Environmental Assessment Registry[2].

It is recommended that, in keeping with the government's adoption of open government principles, GBA+ analysis of final policy decisions be routinely published – either in full or in a streamlined format – at an appropriate phase in the policy cycle, to support a more informed and inclusive debate about policy options. In this regard, the 2017 Gender Statement and the 2018 Equalities Chapter, marked important steps forward. Both included a GBA+ of the government's budget decisions, providing summary information from the GBA+ that were utilised for budget decision making. The 2018 Equalities Chapter also highlighted examples of room for improvement in Budget 2018 GBA+ and committed to publish GBA+ of all budget items starting in Budget 2019.

To further improve transparency in this area, it would be useful for the TBS and SWC to consult with PCO and issue explanatory guidelines regarding the latitude that is available to departments to publish factual GBA+ materials related to announced decisions. Analysis should be presented in a way that is clear and easily understood by all stakeholders including SWC, federal departments, parliament and civil society. The government may wish to develop an online repository where generic gender based analysis and gender-related considerations can be filed for ease of access.

4.2.2. Citizen consultation

Heightened engagement with societal stakeholders is a major trend in modern public governance. According to the 2017 OECD Recommendation on Open Government, it is considered "critical to building citizen trust and is a key contributor to achieving different policy outcomes in diverse domains" (OECD, 2017[42]) .

In line with developments across OECD countries, the government of Canada has increased citizen consultation efforts in recent years. Stakeholders from a broad range of civil society organisations (CSOs), including specific gender equality advocacy groups, report a general improvement in their engagement with government via consultation mechanisms. Some recent examples of good practice in relation to citizen consultation by the Canadian Government are highlighted in Box 4.2.

Box 4.2. Good practice example of citizen engagement in Canada

Employment Insurance Service Quality Review (EI SQR)

Employment Insurance (EI) is a foundational element of Canadians' social safety net and provides temporary income replacement to eligible workers facing job loss, caregiving responsibilities, and sickness, along with maternity and parental leave benefits. In 2015, challenges accessing EI services were causing stress and frustration for many citizens. In response, the government launched a Service Quality Review (EI SQR) nationwide consultation process. This was led by three members of Parliament. Consultations took place in summer 2016 and included site visits, town hall meetings and an on-line survey. The breadth of the consultations undertaken by the Panel was very extensive. Government officials administering the EI programme were encouraged to participate in the on-line survey to ensure their perspective and experiences were also considered. A summary report of feedback received through these consultations was made publicly available. The Review Panel also used the information gleaned from the consultations to develop a number of recommendations to improve the quality of service for the EI program. These recommendations were discussed with stakeholders and further refined.

Source: (Government of Canada,(n.d.)[43])

Innovation, Science and Economic Development Department gender consultations

The Department of Innovation, Science and Economic Development decided to undertake a consultation exercise in 2016 to better understand how it could develop policies to improve gender equality. The department started the exercise by identifying a set of experts who could help with the consultation by acting as engagement leaders. The group consisted of 50% women and 50% men and included a number of stakeholders such as social innovators, venture capitalists and aboriginal business leaders. These engagement leaders undertook consultation events throughout Canada using their own networks. The department found that the information obtained from the consultation exercise was different from what they usually hear. The views challenged the department to think about new initiatives for women, and different groups of women, e.g., that would encourage more entrepreneurs. The department reported that the consultation has informed more inclusive policy development and recent budget proposals.

Source: (Government of Canada, 2018[44])

It's Time: Canada's Strategy to Prevent and Address Gender-Based Violence (GBV)

In 2017, the Government of Canada launched *It's Time: Canada's Strategy to Prevent and Address Gender-Based Violence*. The strategy builds on current federal initiatives, coordinates existing programs, and sets the foundation for greater action on GBV. Through roundtables, meetings, surveys and online submissions, Canadians from various backgrounds (such as Indigenous women, individuals from LGBTQ2 and gender non-conforming communities, young women, women with disabilities, men and women working to end GBV, and newcomers to Canada) shared their experiences and insights. In June 2016, the Minister of Status of Women formed an Advisory Council to serve as a forum to exchange views, share practices, and discuss research related to GBV. A broad range of members were selected for the Advisory Council based on their expertise in violence prevention, LGBTQ2 issues, cyber violence, sexual violence, violence against people with disabilities, violence against Indigenous women and girls, best practices for engaging men and boys, and the criminal justice system.

Source: (Government of Canada, 2017[45])

The government can build on recent improvements through engaging in more systematic citizen consultation and ensuring it is meaningful for citizens. In particular, departments can build structured channels for stakeholder consultation; and create opportunities for citizen input into economic policy and GBA+, which are currently regarded as limited.

The OECD 2017 Recommendation of the Council on Open Government sets out that government should "grant all stakeholders equal and fair opportunities to be informed and consulted and actively engage them in all phases of the policy-cycle and service design and delivery"[3]. It is particularly useful for consultations to begin at the early stages of the policy and budget-making process, when stakeholders still have an opportunity to influence policy design. In addition, the development of feedback mechanisms from departments to citizens in relation to their engagement can help give stakeholders an understanding of the value and relevance of the consultative exercise.

Some stakeholders within public administration spoke of citizen consultation being a "luxury" in a time-constrained work environment. For their part, many CSOs, including gender equality advocacy groups also have logistical and resource issues which constrain their participation in consultation exercises. Some CSOs noted that in order to justify and sustain their engagement, it would be helpful to have a clearer sense of the role, purpose and serious intent of these consultations. Giving CSOs adequate notice of consultation events, support in relation to travel costs and flexibility in terms of how input is delivered (e.g. by videoconference) can help ensure stakeholders have equal and fair opportunities to engage. Specific efforts should be dedicated to reaching out to the most relevant, vulnerable, underrepresented, or marginalised groups in society.

Civil society perspectives have the potential to enrich the quality and the responsive character of gender-responsive, inclusive policy making. CSOs and gender equality advocacy groups often have detailed knowledge of the social and cultural barriers to gender equality and to empowering women and girls, particularly with regard to understanding the intersectionalities that are an important feature of the policy landscape in Canada. More systematic consultation with CSOs would allow government policy development to benefit from the knowledge, views and skills of these stakeholders from the outset of the policy development cycle. Rather than being considered a luxury "add-on" to policy making, structured consultations and feedback mechanisms should in general be factored into the processes and timeline for policy development. Broad-based consultation at the beginning of the each government mandate on gender implications of proposed policy directions could help overcome the time constraints of preparing individual policy proposals (as proposed in Section 2.2.5).

In addition, international experience points to the potential benefits to be obtained from ensuring that independent work to promote gender equality is adequately valued and resourced, to ensure that civil society perspectives can play an effective role in inclusive policy making (see Box 4.3). In this respect, the Budget 2018 measure providing $100 million funding over five years for the Women's Program in order to support initiatives that build the capacity of equality-seeking organisations represents a positive step forward.

Box 4.3. Development funding for women's organisations in the case of the Netherlands

The long-term sustainability of women's empowerment work depends, to a great extent, on the existence and capacity of women's organisations dedicated to the gender equality agenda. This was recognised by the Dutch Ministry of Development Cooperation and in 2008 it dedicated EUR 82 million to the third of the Millennium Development Goals – promoting gender equality and empowering women.

The funding was targeting towards women's rights and civil society organisations to improve the position of women worldwide over a period of four years. A study by the Association for Women's Rights in Development on the impact of the funding, found that it; expanded the outreach and coverage of their work, helped launch new programmes, strategies and initiatives, strengthened their movements and their ability to influence the gender perspectives of other movements and resulted in advocacy successes, including holding onto past gains and preventing the adoption of policies detrimental to women and other marginalised groups.

Source: (Batliwala, Rosenhek and Miller, 2013[46])

Given its leadership role and mandate on gender equality and related issues, it may be advisable to for SWC to establish an advisory panel of experts from civil society, based on the clear and transparent criteria, to help inform strategic choices. This approach would help bridge the gap between government and civil society, help root the actions of SWC in local realities and foster trust in society that views and interests of diverse gender groups are respected. Some international examples are provided in Box 4.4.

Box 4.4. Use of expert panels for dialogue with civil society

Spain's Council for Women's Participation

In Spain, the Council for Women's Participation was established by article 78 of the Constitutional Act 3/2007 of 22 March. The Council is made up of representatives from central, regional and local government as well as women's advocacy organisations. Its role is to channel women's participation in public policy development in relation to the principle of equal treatment and opportunities for women and men. The Government of Spain consults with the Council during the development of the Equal Opportunities Strategic Plan. The Council sets up working groups which focus on different elements of the draft Plan and agree specific amendments aimed at its improvement.

Source: Government of Spain 2018

Sweden's Gender Equality Council

A Swedish Gender Equality Council, convened by the Minister for Gender Equality, has existed since 1982. The Council is made up of representatives from over 50 nationwide organisations that work with gender equality issues. Parliament members are also part of the Council. It convenes three to four times a year and serves as a forum for information, discussion and consultation on current gender equality issues. In spring 2014, the Government's work with the Beijing Platform for Action was presented at the meeting of the Gender Equality Council.

Source: (Government of Sweden, 2014[47])

Ontario's Stakeholder Roundtables

The Ontario Ministry of the Status of Women (MSW) plays an important role across the Ontario Public Service in applying gender analysis to many government actions, and in encouraging partner Ministries to consider gender impacts when developing policies and programs. MSW has created Stakeholder Roundtables so that it can work closely with external stakeholders, partners and experts and receive regular feedback and analysis of the gender impacts of government actions. For example, the Ontario Roundtable on Violence Against Women has been providing advice to the government on initiatives to address gender-based violence since it was established in 2015. The Roundtable is made up of over 20 provincial organisations directly and indirectly involved in violence prevention, public education, human rights and service provision to survivors.

Source: Ontario Ministry of the Status of Women 2018

Australia's National Women's Alliances

In 2010, after an extensive consultation, the Australian Government funded six National Women's Alliances by the amount of $2 million Australian Dollars over three years, a step that signalled a new direction in forming collaborative relationships between women's organisations and the government. This included, for the first time, representation of Indigenous women under their own National Women's Alliance. These six National Women's Alliances (the Alliances) represent almost 120 women's organisations. They bring forward the views, voices and issues of Australian women and, in particular, women from marginalised and disadvantaged groups. The Alliances take the lead in ensuring that the voices of as many women as possible are heard, especially those who in the past have found it difficult to engage in advocacy and decision making. The Alliances are made up of a mix of issues-based and sector-based women's groups each with a distinct focus and a strong capacity for networking and advocacy activities.

Source: (Australian Government,(n.d.)[48])

4.3. Accountability for gender equality through the parliament and the supreme audit institution

4.3.1. The Parliament of Canada

The Parliament of Canada is composed of the Senate, whose members are appointed by the Governor General on the recommendation of the Prime Minister, and the House of Commons, whose members are elected by citizens in general elections. In the most recent election, a record number of women were elected to the current (42nd) House of Commons. However, women still represent just 28% of members. With the decision to appoint a gender equal Cabinet (see Section 1.2.1), the number of women among remaining "back-bench" members is relatively low; and arising from this, committees in the House of Commons are heavily male-dominated. For example, there are just two women on the 12 member House of Commons Standing Committee on Finance (FINA).

Despite the low level of women's representation, the agenda of gender equality and inclusion is a top-level political priority in Canada, and there are strong advocates for this agenda among members in both houses. Parliamentary stakeholders report an increasing interest, among parliamentarians more generally, in the distributional impact of policies.

Parliament's role in gender accountability

The parliament's committees are responsible for reviewing the detail of new and existing legislation and for monitoring the activities of government by conducting reviews of, and inquiries into, programmes and policies, expenditure and appointments. The House of Commons Standing Committee on the Status of Women (FEWO) has the broad authority to study work related to the status of women (House of Commons Canada,(n.d.)[49]). Bills can be referred to the FEWO Committee, although there is no requirement for its involvement in studying bills on a systematic basis, especially those that are not explicitly seen as dealing with the women's issues. The Committee also has autonomy to conduct its own studies. Overall, the Committee is not bound by specific Orders of Reference that determine its work programme, however Committee members have taken a strategic approach in deciding what work to cover. When not dealing with legislation, the Committee has chosen to focus its study on three key areas; gender-based assessment, gender violence and women's economic security.

Beyond FEWO, some parliamentary committees also incorporate a gender element into their work programme. For example, the House of Commons Standing Committee on Public Accounts and the Standing Senate Committee on Human Rights have recently examined the implementation of GBA+ in their respective areas. Also in March 2017, SWC tabled an interim progress report on the implementation of GBA+ to the Public Accounts Committee, to be followed by a final report in 2018.

However, in general, a gender perspective is not mainstreamed through parliamentary committee work, as in other jurisdictions, such as Sweden and the EU (see Box 4.5). Where committees have shown interest in the gender impact of legislative proposals (including those not having an explicit link to gender issues but which may implicitly reinforce remaining inequalities), uncertainty about the boundaries between the principles of transparency, parliamentary scrutiny and the respect for Cabinet confidences, has inhibited full engagement with the factual GBA+ material (see Section 4.2.1 above). The limited incorporation of a gender perspective in committee scrutiny has led to a feeling among CSOs and gender equality advocacy groups that gender issues are often overlooked by parliamentary committees.

It would appear that parliamentary accountability for gender equality and impact is not as robust or systematic as it could be across the wide spectrum of legislative proposals. Giving FEWO a strengthened mandate that includes examination of the gender impact of different legislative proposals (beyond those directly linked to women's issues) could help address this. Improved transparency on GBA+ relating to new legislation and policy proposals (as discussed in Section 4.2.1) would also facilitate this more in-depth accountability function.

A strategic approach where FEWO focuses on legislation that is significant and impactful would help ensure that legislative proposals stand up to challenge for the extent to which they are gender-sensitive. In undertaking this work, there is scope for FEWO to strengthen collaboration and coordination with committees responsible for reviewing the bill, feeding in its assessment in a timely manner.

In addition, parliamentary committees should also be encouraged to mainstream gender considerations in their work (for example, through scrutinising the GBA+ assessment associated with legislative proposals they are examining).

Box 4.5. Gender mainstreaming in parliamentary committee scrutiny

Sweden

The Swedish Parliament (Riksdag) introduced gender mainstreaming in 1994. This means that a gender equality perspective should be taken into account by the Rikstag and its committees in all scrutiny of the executive. All new legislation should be accompanied by an analysis of the impact they will have on men and women. Thus, when parliament committees are examining legislation, they are able to take into account its impact on men and women and use this information to make a more informed decision when they vote on whether or not the proposal should go ahead. Gender has also been mainstreamed into budget scrutiny, with the Committee for Finance examining the annual budget for gender equality aspects as a matter of course.

European Union

The European Parliament's 2003 resolution on gender mainstreaming committed it to incorporating a gender equality perspective in all policies and activities (European Parliament, $2003_{[50]}$). The Committee on Women's Rights and Gender Equality (FEMM Committee) is the main body in charge of promoting gender equality and gender mainstreaming in all the parliament's policy and legislative processes. It coordinates a Gender Mainstreaming Network, which is composed of parliamentarians from each parliamentary committee who are responsible for bringing gender mainstreaming into their committee work. A practice of using "gender mainstreaming amendments" to integrate the gender aspect in the reports of other committees was also introduced at the beginning of the 7th legislative term and continues to be applied.

Source: (European Parliament, $2016_{[51]}$)

Committee evidence-gathering and gender balance

Parliamentary committees often call on experts to give written and oral evidence that will help them hold the government to account publicly for its policies and their implementation. These experts provide an important source of external input into parliamentary scrutiny and, ultimately, public policy.

Although FEWO regularly engages with civil society, gender equality advocacy groups and other stakeholders, there remains room for improvement when it comes to witnesses giving evidence to parliamentary committees as a whole[4]. On the one hand, the gender balance of committee witnesses is influenced by extent to which there is gender equality among experts in a particular field. However, on the other hand, gender equality advocacy groups report that they are often unaware of committee calls for evidence, and even when they submit evidence, they get few invitations to participate in committee hearings. For example, some gender equality advocacy groups expressed disappointment that the FINA Committee does not routinely seek their inputs on public finance or economic issues, although such groups feel that they have relevant expertise.

Ensuring a degree of diversity among experts who give evidence to committees, in terms of gender, but also ethnicity, sexuality, disability, etc., helps to ensure that policy making is fully informed by the range of experiences facing Canadians, and that persistent policy gaps are highlighted and exposed to challenge.

Parliamentary committees could consider additional steps to engage more proactively with a diverse set of stakeholders, representing interests of both women and men from various backgrounds in the consultation process. This may involve publicising calls for evidence more broadly and in a standardised manner (including also social media); considering alternative ways to gather evidence; setting milestones for increasing the proportion of witnesses from underrepresented groups of society; and monitoring progress under these headings. The Parliament of Canada might learn from the efforts of the Scottish Parliament in this area (see Box 4.6).

Box 4.6. Improving gender and representation among committee witnesses in Scotland

The Scottish Parliament's Committee Office commissioned the parliament's information centre (SPICe) and an academic at the University of Lincoln to examine the diversity of committee witnesses and make recommendations on how the diversity of evidence heard by committees might be better recorded, and how it might in some instances be enhanced by engagement with a broader range of voices. The research was published in February 2018 and identified the following possible actions for parliament:

1. Producing guidance for committees on the processes of selecting witnesses and issuing calls for written evidence.
2. Producing guidance for organisations providing witnesses to committees.
3. Improving (online) access to documentation for (particularly first-time) witnesses.
4. Improving support for (particularly first-time) witnesses.
5. Careful assessment of the representativeness of "representative" bodies.
6. Consistent recording of the gender of witnesses (and, potentially, other protected characteristics), which would provide valuable information.
7. Recording informal meetings and similar events in the reports of enquiries.
8. Ensuring that there is sufficient time in each enquiry, where possible, for written evidence to be considered before the selection of invitees to give oral evidence.
9. Exploring the potential benefits of emerging technology as a tool to increase witness diversity.
10. Providing feedback to the witnesses.
11. Monitoring the impact of these changes.

Source: (Bochel and Berthier, 2018[52])

The Library of the Parliament of Canada and gender equality

The Library of the Parliament is the main information repository and research resource for the Parliament of Canada. It provides parliamentarians with news, reference, research and analysis services so that they have the information they need to examine the issues of the day, consider legislation and hold the government to account. In line with this, the Library is responsible for providing parliamentarians with research capacity and data to support their work the area of gender equality.

The Library has been relatively proactive in the area of gender equality. For example, in advance of the Government of Canada's 6th annual GBA+ Awareness Week, the Library released a publication on "Gender-based Analysis Plus in Canada". In recent years, the Library has expanded its ability to respond in area of gender equality. Library staff have also produced a number of research publications on gender issues, and have been encouraged to apply a gender lens to all of their publications, including legislative summaries of private members' bills. Furthermore, Library staff aim to be cognisant of the need for gender balance when providing potential witness lists for committees.

4.3.2. Office of the Auditor General of Canada (OAG)

The Office of the Auditor General of Canada (OAG) provides parliament with objective, fact-based information and expert advice on government programmes and activities, gathered through audits. It carries out three main types of legislative audits: financial audits, performance audits and special examinations.

In April 2008, the FEWO Committee recommended that the OAG examine the implementation of gender-based analysis in the federal government (House of Commons Canada, 2008$_{[53]}$). In response, the OAG undertook focussed audits in relation to gender-based analysis in both 2009 and 2015. These helped shed light on its application across government (see Section 3.2 for details) and also helped mobilise action on the part of key stakeholders to drive improvements. For example, in response to the 2015 audit, SWC, the PCO and TBS tabled the Action Plan on Gender-based Analysis (2016-2020)[5], committing to identify and assess barriers to GBA+ implementation, enhance capacity-building tools and training, and develop monitoring and accountability mechanisms.

Having developed this work stream, the OAG is now one of few supreme audit institutions across the OECD that have conducted audit of gender-based analysis. The strong public and political response to these audits, relative to other audits by the OAG, has been notable, with parliamentary committees holding multiple hearings to discuss the findings. The OAG has shown itself to be a key driver of progress in relation to the application of gender-based analysis, and its continued involvement through focused audits in this area would support the quality of GBA+. These audits could be strengthened if the OAG were able to freely access the GBA+ assessments accompanying policy proposals. The OAG does not currently have access to Cabinet confidences, however, access to the précis accompanying Treasury Board submissions would also allow the OAG to assess fully if TBS is performing its challenge role. Expanding the scope of GBA+ audits to cover implementation and evaluation steps (as is the case in Andalusia in Spain, see Box 4.7) would give greater insights into the extent to which GBA+ is maintained throughout the policy cycle. In light of the independence of the OAG and the need to prioritise its operations in light of resources available, a stronger and clear legislative footing for gender equality institutions and processes – as proposed in Section 3.2 of this report – would strengthen the rationale and the impetus for the OAG to re-orient its operations in this direction, as distinct from standalone or *ad hoc* exercises.

Box 4.7. Gender audits in Andalusia, Spain

Law 18/2003 on Fiscal and Administrative Measures made it compulsory to promote gender audits within the Andalusian Public Administration. Since this time, the Andalusian Regional Government Administration has understood and designed its own gender audits as tools to assess the progress achieved in implementing its gender responsive budgeting strategy.

In 2013, as part of its gender responsive budgeting (GRB) strategy, the Government launched a new series of gender audits. The specific objectives pursued by these audits are to:

1. Assess the extent to which the objectives assigned to budget programmes classed as gender-relevant ("G+") have been attained;
2. Analyse and measure the extent to which gender mainstreaming has been implemented in budget planning, implementation and accountability;
3. Assess the strategies carried out by the managing centres to implement the methodology and achieve their targets; and
4. Identify best practices and make recommendations to strengthen GRB within the Andalusian Public Administration.

These audits are undertaken by the Gender Budgeting Impact Commission, established as part of Law 18/2003. The audits aim to identify progress achieved, lessons learned and insights into how the implementation of gender-relevant budget programmes could be further improved so that they meet their objectives. Draft gender audits are put out for public consultation for a specific length of time in order to take account of any feedback from citizens.

Source: (Andalusian Regional Government Administration, 2014[54])

The OAG could also build on their successful interventions in the area of GBA+ through greater incorporation of a gender perspective across other areas of its work. Ideally, performance audits where there is a gender perspective would be able to consider the extent to which policies and programmes delivered the gender objectives originally anticipated. The OAG could learn from the Austrian Court of Audit in this regard (see Box 4.8).

Box 4.8. Gender dimension to performance audit by the Austrian Court of Audit

The Austrian Court of Audit is the supreme audit institution for Austria, responsible for both financial and performance audits.

Internal guidelines specify that each performance audit should consider complementary questions in the area of gender equality. This includes questions such as:

- Is the gender objective relevant?
- Is there sufficient gender-specific data?
- How appropriate is the level of ambition for measures and indicators?
- What is the impact on society?
- Are women and men appropriately represented in the governing bodies?

For example, an audit of "Agricultural Investment Subsidies and its Outcomes" as part of Austria's rural development programme found that gender equality was not systematically covered by the programme, just 30% of the monitoring committee members were women (despite rules of procedure aimed at gender balanced representation), gender specific investment needs were not analysed despite women predominantly having smaller farms than men, and programme data was not systematically reported and analysed from a gender perspective.

Other recent ACA audits with a gender perspective include: Gender Health in Austria (2015), Compensatory Allowances under Pension Insurance (2015), The Introduction of Outcome Orientation in Selected Federal Ministries (2016), and Gender Aspects in Income Tax Law (2017).

Source: Austrian Court of Audit 2018

In the longer term, as more gender performance objectives become embedded in the programmes of government, the OAG would ideally be able to integrate gender considerations into more, or even all, of its performance audit work, in the same way that an environmental perspective has been integrated in its performance audits, known as the "4th E" (see Box 4.9). This would help enable the OAG fulfil its commitment to contributing, through its audit work and consistent with its mandate, to the federal government's implementation of the SDGs, including Goal 5 relating to Gender Equality[6].

Any development in this respect would need to be accompanied with appropriate guidance, communications and training to ensure that it does not become a mere tick-box exercise.

Box 4.9. Performance audit in Canada and the "4th E"

The Auditor General's responsibilities regarding environmental matters increased with the creation of the position of Commissioner of the Environment and Sustainable Development (CESD) in 1995. The CESD is responsible for monitoring sustainable development strategies of federal departments, overseeing the environmental petitions process, and auditing the federal government's management of environmental and sustainable development issues.

Economy, efficiency, and effectiveness have always been known as the three E's of performance auditing. In 1995, amendments to the Auditor General Act added a fourth E: the environment.

When conducting an audit, the auditor may ask the following questions:

- Has money been spent with due regard to economy?
- Has money been spent with due regard to efficiency?
- Are procedures in place to measure and report on the effectiveness of programmes?
- **Has money been spent with due regard to the effects on the environment?**

The 4th E is contained in section 7(2)(f) of the Auditor General Act, which establishes the OAG's mandate to conduct performance audits and report findings to Parliament.

Source: (Office of the Auditor General of Canada,(n.d.)[55])

Notes

1 For example, Oxfam Canada has recently developed a Feminist Scorecard which they use to review actions taken and progress made against government commitments to gender equality. For more details see https://www.oxfam.ca/turning-feminist-promises-into-progress.

2 See - http://www.ceaa-acee.gc.ca/050/index-eng.cfm

3 For more detail, see 2017 OECD Recommendation of the Council on Open Government: http://www.oecd.org/gov/Recommendation-Open-Government-Approved-Council-141217.pdf

4 The approximate gender breakdown provided by the House of Commons for committees is 33% female witnesses and 66% male witnesses. The Senate reported that approximately 34% of witness salutations in the first session of the 42nd parliament were female (Library of Parliament 2018).

5 See http://cfc-swc.gc.ca/gba-acs/plan-action-2016-en.html

6 See the Sustainable Development Strategy for the Office of the Auditor General of Canada: 2017–2020 - http://www.oag-bvg.gc.ca/internet/English/acc_rpt_e_42863.html

References

Andalusian Regional Government Administration (2014), *PROGRESS IN THE ANDALUSIAN GRB INITIATIVE: GENDER AUDITS*, https://www.wu.ac.at/fileadmin/wu/d/i/vw3/Session_3_Cirujano_Gualda_Romero.pdf (accessed on 17 May 2018). [54]

Australian Government((n.d.)), *National Women's Alliances | Department of the Prime Minister and Cabinet*, 2018, https://www.pmc.gov.au/office-women/grants-and-funding/national-womens-alliances (accessed on 17 May 2018). [48]

Batliwala, S., S. Rosenhek and J. Miller (2013), "WOMEN MOVING MOUNTAINS: COLLECTIVE IMPACT OF THE DUTCH MDG3 FUND HOW RESOURCES ADVANCE WOMEN'S RIGHTS AND GENDER EQUALITY", https://www.awid.org/sites/default/files/atoms/files/Women%20Moving%20Mountains.pdf. [46]

Bochel, H. and A. Berthier (2018), *SPICe Briefing: Committee witnesses: gender and representation*, https://sp-bpr-en-prod-cdnep.azureedge.net/published/2018/2/27/Committee-witnesses--gender-and-representation/SB%2018-16.pdf (accessed on 17 May 2018). [52]

Bohnet, I. (2016), *What works: Gender Equality by Design*, Harvard University Press. [16]

Canadian Feminist Alliance for International Action (FAFIA) (2016), *Because its 2016! A National Gender Equality Plan*, http://tbinternet.ohchr.org/Treaties/CEDAW/Shared%20Documents/CAN/INT_CEDAW_NGO_CAN_25417_E.pdf (accessed on 12 December 2017). [23]

Canadian Institute for Advanced Research & Vancouver School of Economics (2016), *Earnings Inequality and the Gender Pay Gap*, http://faculty.arts.ubc.ca/nfortin/Fortin_EarningsInequalityGenderPayGap.pdf. [6]

Catalyst (2017), *Women In Male-Dominated Industries And Occupations*, http://www.catalyst.org/knowledge/women-male-dominated-industries-and-occupations. [10]

Congressional Budget Office (2016), *CBO's 2016 Long-Term Projections for Social Security: Additional Information*, https://www.cbo.gov/sites/default/files/114th-congress-2015-2016/reports/52298-socialsecuritychartbook.pdf. [62]

Downes, R., L. Von Trapp and S. Nicol (2016), "Gender budgeting in OECD countries", *OECD Journal on Budgeting* 3, http://www.oecd.org/gender/Gender-Budgeting-in-OECD-countries.pdf. [59]

EIGE (2018), *Spain – Structures*, http://eige.europa.eu/gender-mainstreaming/countries/spain/structures. [27]

European Parliament (2016), *Report on Gender Mainstreaming in the work of the European Parliament - A8-0034/2016*, http://www.europarl.europa.eu/sides/getDoc.do?type=REPORT&reference=A8-2016- [51]

0034&language=EN (accessed on 17 May 2018).

European Parliament (2003), *European Parliament resolution on gender mainstreaming in the European Parliament (2002/2025(INI))*, http://www.europarl.europa.eu/sides/getDoc.do?pubRef=-//EP//TEXT+TA+P5-TA-2003-0098+0+DOC+XML+V0//EN. [50]

Flumian, M. (2016), "What Trudeau's committees tell us about his government | Institute on Governance", *Institute on Governance*, https://iog.ca/research-publications/publications/what-trudeaus-committees-tell-us-about-his-government/ (accessed on 21 January 2018). [29]

Goldin, C. (2014), "A Grand Gender Convergence: Its Last Chapter", *American Economic Review*, Vol. 104/4, pp. 1091-1119. [5]

Government of Canada (2018), *Budget 2018: Equality + Growth, A Strong Middle Class*, https://www.budget.gc.ca/2018/docs/plan/budget-2018-en.pdf. [8]

Government of Canada (2018), *Budget Plan + Growth*, https://financebudget.azurewebsites.net/2018/docs/plan/chap-01-en.html?wbdisable=true. [7]

Government of Canada (2018), *Innovation, Science and Economic Development Canada - Canada.ca*, https://www.canada.ca/en/innovation-science-economic-development.html. [44]

Government of Canada (2018), *Mandate Letter Tracker: Delivering results for Canadians*, https://www.canada.ca/en/privy-council/campaigns/mandate-tracker-results-canadians.html (accessed on 10 February 2018). [33]

Government of Canada (2018), *Policy on Results*, https://www.tbs-sct.gc.ca/pol/doc-eng.aspx?id=31300 (accessed on 17 May 2018). [38]

Government of Canada (2017), *Budget 2017: Building a Strong Middle Class*, https://www.budget.gc.ca/2017/docs/plan/budget-2017-en.pdf. [57]

Government of Canada (2017), *Fact Sheet: It's time to pay attention*, http://www.swc-cfc.gc.ca/violence/strategy-strategie/fs-fi-3-en.html. [45]

Government of Canada (2017), *Multilateral Early Learning and Child Care Framework - Canada.ca*, https://www.canada.ca/en/employment-social-development/programs/early-learning-child-care/reports/2017-multilateral-framework.html (accessed on 11 December 2017). [24]

Government of Canada (2017), *Results and Delivery in Canada: Building on momentum*, http://www.fmi.ca/media/1200856/results_and_delivery_building_momentum_october_2017.pdf. [34]

Government of Canada (2016), *Fall Economic Statement 2016*, https://www.budget.gc.ca/fes-eea/2016/docs/statement-enonce/fes-eea-2016-eng.pdf. [56]

Government of Canada (2016), *Increasing Recruitment of Women into the Canadian Armed Forces*. [17]

Government of Canada((n.d.)), *Charter Statements - Canada's System of Justice*, 2018, http://www.justice.gc.ca/eng/csj-sjc/pl/charter-charte/index.html (accessed on 17 May 2018). [41]

Government of Canada((n.d.)), *Employment Insurance Service Quality Review Report: Making Citizens Central*, 2017, https://www.canada.ca/en/employment-social-development/programs/ei/ei-list/reports/service-quality-review-report.html. [43]

Government of Finland (2016), *Government Action Plan For Gender Equality 2016–2019*, https://julkaisut.valtioneuvosto.fi/bitstream/handle/10024/79305/03_2017_Tasa-arvo-ohjelma_Enkku_kansilla.pdf?sequence=1. [19]

Government of Iceland((n.d.)), *Gender Budgeting*, 2018, https://www.government.is/topics/economic-affairs-and-public-finances/gender-budgeting/ (accessed on 16 May 2018). [60]

Government of Spain (2014), *Plan Estratégico de Igualdad de Oportunidades 2014-2016*, http://www.inmujer.gob.es/actualidad/PEIO/docs/PEIO2014-2016.pdf. [20]

Government of Sweden (2014), *Sweden's follow-up of the Platform for Action from the UN's*, https://www.regeringen.se/contentassets/b2f5cc340526433f8e33df3024d510e3/swedens-follow-up-of-the-platform-for-action-from-the-uns-fourth-world-conference-on-women-in-beijing-1995---covering-the-period-between-20092014. [47]

Government of Sweden (2007), *Moving Ahead: Gender budgeting in Sweden*, http://store1.digitalcity.eu.com/store/clients/release/AAAAGNJH/doc/gender-budgeting-in-sweden_2007.09.29-12.22.48.pdf. [65]

House of Commons Canada (2008), *Committee Report No. 9 - FEWO (39-2) - House of Commons of Canada*, http://www.ourcommons.ca/DocumentViewer/en/39-2/FEWO/report-9/. [53]

House of Commons Canada (2007), *Report of the Standing Committee on the Status of Women: The impacts of funding and program changes at Status of Women Canada*, http://www.ourcommons.ca/Content/Committee/391/FEWO/Reports/RP2876038/feworp18/feworp18-e.pdf (accessed on 23 January 2018). [26]

House of Commons Canada((n.d.)), *FEWO - About*, 2018, https://www.ourcommons.ca/Committees/en/FEWO/About (accessed on 17 May 2018). [49]

IMF (2017), *Gender Budgeting in G7 Countries*, https://www.imf.org/en/Publications/Policy-Papers/Issues/2017/05/12/pp041917gender-budgeting-in-g7-countries. [36]

Mahony, T. (2011), "Women and the Criminal Justice System", *Statistics Canada Catalogue no. 89-503-X*, http://www.statcan.gc.ca/pub/89-503-x/2010001/article/11416-eng.pdf (accessed on 17 May 2018). [11]

McInturff, K. and B. Lambert (2016), *Making Women Count: The Unequal Economics of Women's Work*, | Canadian Centre for Policy Alternatives, OXFAM Canada, https://www.policyalternatives.ca/publications/reports/making-women-count-0 (accessed on 01 January 2018). [13]

McKinsey Global Institute (2017), *The power of parity: Advancing women's equality in Canada,* https://www.mckinsey.com/featured-insights/gender-equality/the-power-of-parity-advancing-womens-equality-in-canada (accessed on 16 May 2018). [2]

Moyser, M. (2017), *Women and Paid Work, Statistics Canada, March, available online at: http://www.statcan.gc.ca/pub/89-503-x/2015001/article/14694-eng.htm.* [4]

OECD (2017), *Behavioural Insights and Public Policy: Lessons from Around the World.*, OECD Publishing. [15]

OECD (2017), *Building an inclusive Mexico : Policies and Good Governance for Gender Equality,* OECD Publishing. [28]

OECD (2017), *Recommendation of the Council on Open Government,* http://www.oecd.org/gov/Recommendation-Open-Government-Approved-Council-141217.pdf. [42]

OECD (2017), *The Pursuit of Gender Equality: An Uphill Battle*, OECD Publishing, Paris, http://dx.doi.org/10.1787/9789264281318-en. [1]

OECD (2016), *Open Government The Global Context and the Way Forward*, OECD Publishing. [32]

OECD (2016), "Open Government: The Global Context and The Way Forward", http://www.oecd-ilibrary.org/docserver/download/4216481e.pdf?expires=1516890637&id=id&accname=ocid84004878&checksum=36020513E75CAF56257B41F9DC2A3AFC (accessed on 25 January 2018). [31]

OECD (2015), "Delivering from the Centre: Strengthening the role of the centre of government in driving priority strategies", https://www.oecd.org/gov/cog-2015-delivering-priority-strategies.pdf (accessed on 21 January 2018). [25]

OECD (Forthcoming), *Budgeting in Austria.* [37]

OECD (Forthcoming), *Budgeting Outlook 2018.* [39]

OECD (Forthcoming), *Budgeting Practices and Procedures Dataset.* [58]

OECD (Forthcoming), *Governance Guidelines for Gender Budgeting.* [64]

OECD (forthcoming) (2018), *OECD Economic Surveys: Canada, OECD Publishing, Paris.* [3]

Office of the Auditor General Canada (2016), *Implementing Gender-Based Analysis,* http://www.oag-bvg.gc.ca/internet/English/parl_oag_201602_01_e_41058.html (accessed on 24 January 2018). [30]

Office of the Auditor General of Canada((n.d.)), *The Environment and Sustainable Development Guide*, 2018, http://www.oag-bvg.gc.ca/internet/English/meth_lp_e_19275.html (accessed on 17 May 2018). [55]

OXFAM Canada (2017), *Feminist Scorecard 2017: Tracking government action to advance women's rights and gender equality,* http://www.oxfam.ca (accessed on 11 December 2017). [22]

Schratzenstaller, M. (2014), *The implementation of gender responsive budgeting in Austria as* [35] *central element of a major budget reform*, https://www.wu.ac.at/fileadmin/wu/d/i/vw3/Session_4_Schratzenstaller.pdf.

Sharp, R. and R. Broomhill (2013), *A Case Study of Gender Responsive Budgeting in Australia*, https://consultations.worldbank.org/Data/hub/files/grb_papers_australia_updf_final.pdf. [63]

Status of Women Canada (2017), *It's Time: Canada's Strategy To Prevent and Address Gender-based Violence*, Government of Canada, http://www.swc-cfc.gc.ca/violence/strategy-strategie/GBV_Fact_sheets_2.pdf (accessed on 01 January 2018). [12]

Status of Women Canada((n.d.)), *The History of GBA+ Domestic and International Milestones*. [14]

Swedish Fiscal Policy Council (2016), *Finanspolitiska rådets rapport 2016*, http://www.finanspolitiskaradet.com/download/18.21a8337f154abc1a5dd28c15/1463487699296/Svensk+finanspolitik+2016.pdf. [61]

The Victorian Government (2018), *Safe and Strong: A Victorian Gender Equality Strategy. Achievements Report Year One*, https://www.vic.gov.au/system/user_files/Documents/women/1801009_Safe_and_strong_first_year_report_summary_10_%C6%92_web.pdf (accessed on 17 May 2018). [18]

UK National Audit Office (2016), *Sustainability in the spending review*, https://www.nao.org.uk/wp-content/uploads/2016/07/Sustainability-in-the-Spending-Review.pdf. [40]

United Nations (2016), "Concluding observations on the combined eighth and ninth periodic reports of Canada*", https://documents-dds-ny.un.org/doc/UNDOC/GEN/N16/402/03/PDF/N1640203.pdf?OpenElement (accessed on 11 December 2017). [21]

Wells, M. (2018), *Closing the Engineering Gender Gap*, https://www.design-engineering.com/features/engineering-gender-gap/. [9]

Chapter 5. Advancing gender budgeting in Canada

This Chapter assesses the efforts of the Government of Canada so far in relation to gender budgeting and provides recommendations for how developments to date can be built upon to ensure a more effective and sustainable approach. Gender budgeting has only recently been introduced in Canada but is already proving itself to be an influential tool, encouraging departments to think in a more structured way about the design and conduct of GBA+ and to develop policies that help achieve gender results. Significant gender budgeting attention has focussed on the introduction of gender equality-related content in the budget. However, the presentation of this information is just one element of the wide-ranging approach to gender budgeting being developed by Canada. Reviewing the gender impact of baseline spend and strengthening the application of a gender lens to ex post processes such as evaluation and spending review will help ensure that gender budgeting is embedded across the full budget cycle. Parliamentary scrutiny of gender budgeting remains at an under-developed stage, but will be essential to ensure the government is held to account for its actions in this area.

5.1. Introduction

Gender budgeting means the systematic application of analytical tools and processes, as a routine part of the budget process, in order to highlight gender equality issues and to inform, prioritise and resource gender-responsive policies.

The 2015 Recommendation and its implementation Toolkit identify gender budgeting as a key tool of a system-wide government approach to deliver gender equality outcomes. The OECD approach to gender budgeting underlines that this should not be a standalone tool, but should be organically linked with a country's broader gender equality framework (see Chapter 2).

While FIN has incorporated GBA+ into its budget processes since 1995, there has been no specific requirement for expenditure or tax policy measures to be linked with gender equality objectives. With gender equality and inclusiveness identified as over-arching policy principles by the current Government of Canada, FIN announced in 2016 a commitment to introduce gender budgeting. A key feature of FIN's approach to gender budgeting is that it builds on existing strengths of the Canadian system, in particular gender-based analysis. The commitment stated:

"To ensure that the government continues to deliver real and meaningful change for all Canadians, it will submit Budget 2017, and all future budgets, to more rigorous analysis by completing and publishing a gender-based analysis of budgetary measures." (Government of Canada, 2016$_{[56]}$)

This initiative, and its subsequent development, has brought Canada into a group of 16 OECD countries who have already introduced elements of gender budgeting[1]. Canada was among the first wave of G7 countries to implement a gender budgeting approach at the national level. This chapter assesses the nature of the gender budgeting initiative within Canada and offers recommendations for how it could be developed further.

5.2. Implementation of gender budgeting in Canada

5.2.1. Gender budgeting developments so far

When the Government of Canada made the public commitment towards a gender-based analysis of budgetary measures in 2016, the Budget 2017 process was already well underway and FIN had already received letters from the departments with their budget proposals. The gender-based analysis of budgetary measures – i.e. the specific commitment in the 2016 Fall Economic Statement – needed to draw in the first instance upon information provided through existing GBA+ processes and practices. This information was formulated into a "Gender Statement", included as a chapter within the main Budget 2017 publication (March 2017). The Gender Statement was composed of two main elements:

1. **Overview statistics in relation to gender in Canada in 2017**, including an assessment of the gender wage gap, labour market challenges, and the likelihood of experiencing poverty and violence.
2. **A description of measures in Budget 2017 aimed at addressing gender-based challenges**. This chapter-by-chapter summary outlined measures that were focused on advancing gender equality and their anticipated impact, with the information drawn almost exclusively from departmental GBA+.

The initial Gender Statement represented a pragmatic approach to connecting the gender equality agenda with the budget process. It had the advantages of:-

(a) Integrating a gender equality report as a core element of the government's main budget document, rather than as ancillary information,

(b) Drawing upon the extensive corpus of GBA+ material that is routinely generated within Canada's policy making system,

(c) Helping to bring key elements of the GBA+ material into public view, thus promoting a more transparent approach, and

(d) Providing an accountability tool to inform parliamentary and public debate on how the agenda of gender equality is being advanced at the federal level.

In presenting the Gender Statement, the Government of Canada acknowledged that its development was not complete, noting that *"Future Gender Statements will provide more in-depth analysis of proposed budget measures"* and committing the government to *"improve upon this work, and make meaningful progress in elevating gender to the mainstream of government decision-making"* (Government of Canada, 2017[57]).

In preparation for Budget 2018, FIN took a number of steps to improve the gender-based analysis of budget measures in line with its public commitment. In order to further improve the quantity and quality of GBA+ that it had to draw on, the Minister of Finance explicitly referenced the need for clear and rigorous GBA+ in all budget and off-cycle funding proposals in letters to Ministers. The core requirements relating to this development were outlined in instructions distributed to departments explaining the nature of the supporting analysis that should be provided. Importantly, departmental stakeholders reported that these changes have already encouraged them to think in a more structured way about the design and conduct of GBA+ and more profoundly about the potential gender impact of new policies and proposals.

Over the course of the OECD Review, the OECD worked with FIN to further develop the content of the gender statement accompanying Budget 2018, now in the form of an Equality Chapter. Key developments included:

- The introduction of a Gender Results Framework to guide Budget 2018 and future budgets. This provides a whole-of-government tool to measure progress in Canada in relation to gender equality, and to help identify where the greatest gaps remain.
- A more comprehensive GBA+ of budget 2018. This provided information on the key tax and spend measures within each budget chapter and summarised their impact on gender equality, even if the measures were not directly aimed at supporting gender equality.
- The highlighting of areas where there is room for improvement in the GBA+ presented to FIN alongside budget measures, to ensure that that quality of GBA+ presented alongside budget proposals improves and goes beyond a tick box exercise.

These developments further built the momentum for gender budgeting in Canada. In Budget 2018, no budget decision was taken without being informed by GBA+. In addition, government stakeholders reported that the new Gender Results Framework provided a useful framework for policy discussion and helped guide Ministerial decision making in relation to resource allocation.

Canada is now in the position where it presents comprehensive gender information and analysis as part of the budget relative to OECD peers (see Table 5.1).

Table 5.1. Gender information presented as part of the budget across OECD countries

OECD country	Gender objectives	Progress statement in relation to gender objectives	Information on total spending allocated to gender equality projects	Gender impact analysis of specific budget measures	Gender impact analysis of budget as a whole
Canada	●	●		●	●
Iceland				●	
Japan	●		●		
Korea	●	●	●	●	
Mexico	●	●	●	●	●
Portugal	●		●		
Spain	●	●	●	●	●
Sweden			●	●	

Note: Data shown only for the OECD countries which publish gender information alongside the budget.
Source: (OECD, Forthcoming[58])

The Government of Canada is ambitious to continue developing its gender budgeting practice in the years ahead and explicitly stated this in Budget 2018. In line with this commitment, the government has already undertaken to publish GBA+ of all budget items starting in Budget 2019.

Gender equality advocacy groups and other civil society organisations have in general been supportive of the 2017 Gender Statement and 2018 Equalities Chapter, viewing these initiatives as a "bold step forward" for gender equality in Canada. In general terms, civil society stakeholders acknowledge that gender budgeting in Canada is in its early stages and accept at face value, for now, the government's public commitment to undertaking improvements. Most are prepared to reserve judgement about the effectiveness of gender budgeting until the process has been given space to mature. However, the same stakeholders expressed that the test of its effectiveness will be determined ultimately by two factors:

1. The extent to which the gender equality-related content in the budget develops as a political "PR" tool of government versus an accountability tool to further gender equality. The coverage and content of the statement seems crucial to this question. If information is only provided on selected positive measures, the government may be accused of "cherry-picking" the information that it presents. On the other hand, a full and open presentation helps foster public trust and build an understanding of the difficult policy trade-offs with which policy makers and political leaders must sometimes contend.
2. The extent to which gender budgeting acts as a catalyst for important and significant policy developments in the area of gender equality, e.g., in the area of childcare.

Further development of gender equality-related content in the budget

Taking account of the developments to date and the insights and suggestions of various stakeholders in Canada, and of effective international experiences of gender budgeting, further steps that FIN could take to strengthen the comprehensiveness of the GBA+ of the budget would be to:

- Deliver on its commitment to provide information on how all budget measures, including cuts, are anticipated to impact gender equality, drawing on information from the GBA+ that accompany each budget proposal.
- Increase recognition, where possible, of intersectionality and how key budget measures might impact different groups of society, such as Indigenous women, women with disabilities, and different gender identities, where data is available.

FIN could also further strengthen the gender equality-related content presented with budget by:

- Presenting analysis showing the distributional impact of new tax and benefit measures on different groups of women and men. This type of analysis is already undertaken in-house by FIN, but public systematic presentation of this information – as is done in other OECD countries (see Box 5.1) - will help improve transparency. FIN could also present analysis on how the budget impacts incentives for second earners to enter formal employment[2] and the ability of difference groups of women and men to access public services.
- Developing capacity for gender budget tagging to highlight and monitor how much money is disbursed through the budget in order to achieve gender equality goals. This development would not necessarily involve re-engineering of the financial management IT system; it should rather build upon the innovative policy tagging system that is being advanced by the RDU (see Chapter 3).

While incorporating new developments to strengthen the gender-equality-related content in the budget, in the medium-term FIN should aim to develop a standard format and structure, which can be expected to remain broadly stable over time to ensure transparency and facilitate accountability. It may be prudent to present core gender information – such as the Gender Results Framework - and summary analysis in the budget document, while presenting more comprehensive analysis in accompanying material.

Box 5.1. Examples of distributional analysis accompanying the budget

United Kingdom

The UK Government publishes a distributional analysis of the budget's impact on households. This analysis looks at the impact of new measures on different household net income deciles. Where possible, policy changes are analysed using HM Treasury's IntraGovernmental Tax and Benefit microsimulation model.

The distributional analysis includes tax, welfare and public service spending measures implemented since the start of the parliamentary term that carry a direct, quantifiable impact on households. With respect to spending on public services, the cash value spent on the public service is converted into an identical cash gain to households. Where there is insufficient data to robustly model the distributional impact of a measure, it is not included.

Source: (HM Treasury UK, 2017[24])

Ireland

The Government of Ireland publishes a distributional analysis of budget measures on a variety of household family types across a range of income levels. This analysis is undertaken using the Economic and Social Research Institute's SWITCH model and it shows the combined effect of social welfare and tax changes contained in the budget. Distribution tables show the impact of budget measures for different family types – single individuals, married couples, families with children - across a range of income levels.

In 2014, the ESRI and the Equality Authority also co-published a study on the gender impact of tax, welfare and public-sector pay changes. The analysis was based on the ESRI's new Microsimulation Method for Equality Analysis which used the Institute's tax benefit model to assess the impacts of policy changes on men and women, based on a large-scale nationally representative survey. Faced with limited information on how income is shared between couples, the study presented results based on a number of different scenarios.

Sources: (Government of Ireland, 2016[25]) and (Keane Claire, Callan Tim, 2014[25])

5.2.2. Embedding GBA+ approaches across the full budgeting and policy cycle

OECD analysis points to a range of opportunities across the budget cycle in which the gender perspective can be brought to bear (Downes, Von Trapp and Nicol, 2016[59]). Significant gender budgeting attention has focussed on the introduction of gender equality-related content as part of the budget. However, the presentation of this information is just one element of the wide-ranging approach to gender budgeting being developed by Canada (see Figure 5.1).

Figure 5.1. Elements of gender budgeting embedded across the Canadian budget cycle

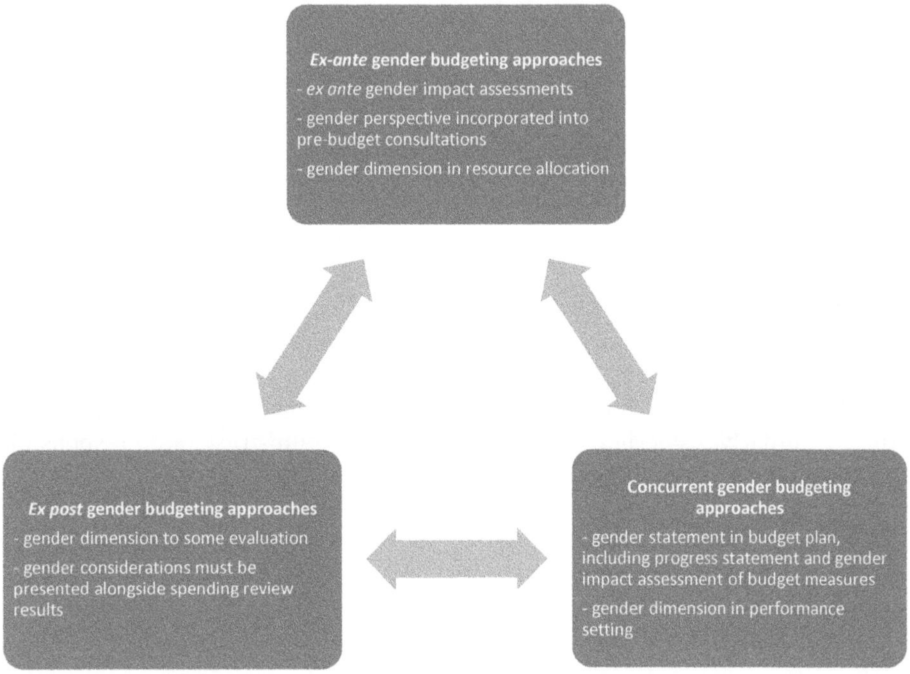

In the Canadian context *ex ante* gender budgeting approaches are relatively well developed thanks to the GBA+ tool and recent efforts to improve its application. The introduction of a gender perspective in pre-budget consultations is also a strength of the Canadian approach (see Section 5.2.4). However, as these efforts focus on incremental budget measures there would be merit in better understanding the gender impact of baseline spending. In recognition of this, in Budget 2018 the government committed to "extending the reach of GBA+ to examine tax expenditures, federal transfers and the existing spending base, including the Estimates" (Government of Canada, 2018[8]).

To take forward this area of work, TBS may wish to work with departments to develop a rolling programme of gender budget baseline analysis. This could involve a set number of "deep dive" exercises each year to identify the gender impact of specific budget programmes. The value of this exercise is only realised if the results are used to inform future policy development and budget decisions. The results of gender budget baseline analyses should also be made public to facilitate citizens holding the government to account for its decisions and to ensure transparency.

In addition, as indicated in Chapters 3 and 4, the introduction of a whole-of-government Gender Results Framework has raised the priority of gender considerations within resource allocation decisions and allows for the tracking of progress against gender equality objectives over time. Gender considerations are also being incorporated into departmental planning and reporting processes. Nevertheless, there is scope to further ensure a gender perspective is incorporated into *ex post* gender budgeting approaches such as evaluations, performance audits and spending review.

It is observed that embedding gender budgeting throughout the budget cycle requires the collective effort of a number of government stakeholders. FIN is well placed to take a leadership role to help mobilise and strengthen the wide range of gender budgeting tools being implemented by different government stakeholders across the budget cycle. By working closely with SWC and other key stakeholders (including PCO, TBS, departments and the OAG) across government, FIN can ensure a comprehensive and coordinated approach to gender budgeting continues to develop. To facilitate this, FIN may consider instituting an inter-agency gender budgeting working group, drawing on models such as Iceland's Gender Budgeting Committee (see Box 5.2). Any working group would need to coordinate closely with cross-departmental GBA+ networks.

Box 5.2. Iceland's Gender Budgeting Committee

Iceland's Gender Budgeting Committee has been set up, and is led by, the Ministry of Finance and Economic Affairs in a formal cooperation with the Ministry of Welfare. The Committee includes representatives of all the ministries and the Centre for Gender Equality. It is responsible for preparing the implementation programme for gender budgeting. Similarly, steering groups in all the ministries are responsible for implementing gender budgeting within each ministry.

Source: (Government of Iceland,(n.d.)[60])

5.2.3. Parliamentary scrutiny of gender budgeting

The 2017 Gender Statement and 2018 Equalities Chapter are well placed to be useful tools of accountability. Subjecting gender equality-related content in the budget to scrutiny by parliamentarians is one of the key potential benefits of this approach, opening the way for substantive engagement with the policy priorities, and reporting of results.

The first year that the Gender Statement was published, neither the FINA Committee, nor the FEWO Committee extended their scrutiny to look at it. In 2018, however, the FEWO Committee took the welcome step of holding its first ever hearing with the Minister for Finance in relation to the impact of Budget 2018 on women and girls. The engagement of the FEWO Committee this scrutiny is a positive step forward. However, scrutiny of gender budgeting remains under-developed relative to practices in other OECD countries where the parliament is observed to be more engaged (see Box 5.3 for the example of Austria). It is not yet clear if there is a fixed "home" for parliamentary scrutiny of equality-related content in the budget, leaving accountability for it in a weak position. In the longer term, a more robust accountability model may involve both the Finance and FEWA Committees holding a joint session to examine the equality impact of the budget. Committee(s) would be expected to engage with the Finance Minister and the Minister for Status of Women, as well as gender equality advocacy groups, in undertaking this scrutiny.

Box 5.3. Parliamentary scrutiny of gender budgeting in Austria

In Austria, gender equality and gender budgeting are an integrated part of the federal budget law and the performance budgeting system. Under each of the 33 budget chapters, Ministers have to define five outcome objectives, with at least one addressing gender equality. Progress is reported in the Annual Federal Performance Report. In general, a high level of interest from the MPs in relation to gender equality is reported. The Budget Committee at the Austrian Parliament scrutinises gender equality objectives as part of its budget oversight. The committee often holds intensive discussions on the objectives, and they are also debated in plenary sessions. MPs often question their relevance, the level of ambition and the availability of adequate funds to achieve them.

Source: (Berger Helmut, 2017[25])

Scrutiny of gender budgeting by the Parliamentary Budget Office (PBO)

The Parliamentary Budget Office (PBO) was established in 2008 to support parliament by providing analysis of macroeconomic and fiscal policy for the purposes of raising the quality of parliamentary debate and promoting greater budget transparency and accountability. It has a mandate to provide independent analysis to parliament on the budget, the estimates and other documents.

In relation to its work on the annual budget proposal, the PBO has not yet engaged in scrutiny of the budget's gender equality-related content. However, it has developed some budget analysis tools that provide independent assessment of how budget measures impact individuals in different circumstances. For example, the PBO has an online tool allowing users to input their income, and other personal details, and get an estimate of the impact that proposed changes will have on their federal monthly benefits, after-tax or disposable income, and their federal income taxes payable. The PBO also incorporates distributional analysis into some of its costings work, particularly where members indicate that they have an interest in this information. It may also occasionally independently assess the validity of analysis the government has produced on the distributional impacts of its proposed measures. However, in general the government does not produce significant material in this respect.

Presently, the PBO has a broad mandate and relatively low staffing by international standards, forcing the office to heavily prioritise how it uses its resources. However, with the PBO in the process of expanding its staffing capacity, the question of engaging more substantively with equality-related content in the budget would appear to be both practicable and appropriate: particularly if parliamentary committees move towards a more structured approach to scrutiny of this in future.

The PBO's independent authority and fiscal expertise would lend themselves well to future assessment of equality-related content in the budget. If the PBO is to engage in this area, a useful starting point may be the provision of independent distributional analysis on the extent to which gender equality is effectively promoted through the tax and benefit policies in the budget proposal has the potential to improve budget transparency and accountability and support broader parliamentary scrutiny of the budget. The PBO may also consider incorporating GBA+ analysis in its reports as part of a standard practice. There are examples of other independent fiscal institutions across the OECD which apply a gender dimension to their work (see Box 5.4).

Box 5.4. Independent fiscal institutions and analysis of gender equality

Swedish Fiscal Policy Council

The Swedish Fiscal Policy Council was established in 2007 as the independent fiscal institution for Sweden. The Government's instruction to the Council asks it to 'analyse the effects of fiscal policy on the distribution of welfare in the short and the long term.' Every year since 1989, the Government's Budget Bill has included an annex on the distribution of economic resources between women and men. This annex is part of Government efforts to change the distribution of resources between women and men. In its 2016 Report, the Council opted to devote a chapter to the scrutiny of this annex. In this chapter, the Council outlines how the annex could be improved to better support Government's objectives in the area of equality policy.

Source: (Swedish Fiscal Policy Council, 2016[61])

US Congressional Budget Office (CBO)

The US CBO produces independent analyses of budgetary and economic issues to support the Congressional budget process. It does not routinely include a gender dimension to its distributional analysis. However, there are some examples where it applies a gender dimension to its work. For example, each year the CBO prepares long-term projections of the federal government's revenues and outlays, including those for the Social Security program. The 2016 projections illustrate the distribution of benefits paid to and payroll taxes collected for men and women, as shown in the table below:

Mean Initial Benefits for Retired Workers, With Scheduled and Payable Benefits

Thousands of 2016 Dollars

10-Year Birth Cohort	All Retired Workers		Lowest Quintile of Lifetime Household Earnings		Middle Quintile of Lifetime Household Earnings		Highest Quintile of Lifetime Household Earnings	
	Scheduled	Payable	Scheduled	Payable	Scheduled	Payable	Scheduled	Payable
All								
1940s	17	17	9	9	18	18	24	24
1960s	19	17	10	9	19	17	27	24
1980s	24	18	13	9	24	17	36	26
2000s	35	25	19	13	34	24	52	37
Men								
1940s	21	21	11	11	22	22	27	27
1960s	21	19	11	10	22	19	30	27
1980s	27	20	14	10	26	19	41	30
2000s	39	27	20	14	38	26	59	41
Women								
1940s	14	14	8	8	14	14	19	19
1960s	17	15	10	9	17	15	23	20
1980s	22	16	12	9	22	16	31	22
2000s	31	22	18	13	31	22	44	31

Source: (Congressional Budget Office, 2016[62])

5.2.4. Developing an effective and sustainable approach to gender budgeting

Gender budgeting presents significant social and economic opportunities for Canada. However, implementing an effective and sustainable gender budgeting approach can be challenging. Some challenges derive from the differing levels of importance given to gender equality by successive governments (see Box 5.5 for the experience in Australia), whereas others relate more broadly to the challenges faced when implementing any new practice or procedure in government.

Box 5.5. The rise and fall of gender budgeting in Australia

The Government of Australia was considered a "pioneer" of gender budgeting when it included a Women's Budget Statement as part of the 1984/85 budget documents. By the late 1980s the Women's Budget Statement became part of an integrated approach, which included the development of a National Agenda for Women.

Over subsequent years, however, the Women's Budget Statement came to be viewed as an exercise internal to the bureaucracy, and of little relevance to the women's movement. Political and administrative championing of the Women's Budget Statement fell away, and the document was dramatically downsized in budgets 1994–95 and 1995–96.

Following the election of a new government in 1996, the Women's Budget Statement was effectively discontinued at the federal level; and the concept of gender budgeting in Australia has retained ideological and political associations which have hindered its re-emergence as a 'neutral' and broadly-supported tool of modern policy making.

Source: (Sharp and Broomhill, 2013[63])

An OECD publication on Governance Guidelines for Gender Budgeting (OECD, Forthcoming[64]) presents essential elements to help to successfully embed a gender perspective within the Public Financial Management framework, a number of which are relevant to the Canadian context. These include:

- Providing legal foundations for gender budgeting;
- Building a corpus of gender-disaggregated data;
- The Department of Finance as an advocate for gender budgeting;
- Ensuring gender budgeting is open to critical perspectives; and
- Measuring the impact of gender budgeting.

Proposed directions for advancing these elements in Canada are provided in the following paragraphs.

Providing legal foundations for gender budgeting

Legislation that is fully tested and debated in parliament can help embed gender budgeting as a valued and enduring feature of public policy making and insulate it, as far as possible, from fluctuations arising from the economic or political environment. Gender budgeting has legal underpinning in half of the OECD countries where it is practiced (see Figure 5.2). The nature and objectives of the legal provisions for gender budgeting vary in line with country-specific circumstances.

Figure 5.2. Legal foundations for gender budgeting across OECD countries

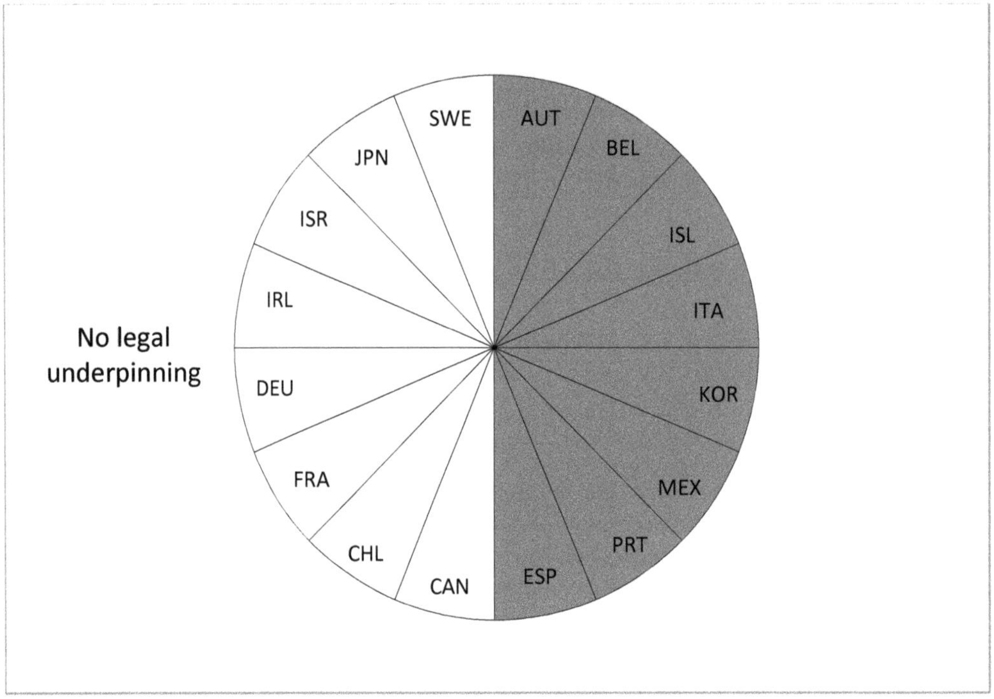

Note: Shows data only for OECD countries where gender budgeting is practised.
Source: (OECD, Forthcoming[58])

In Canada's case, with a Westminster model of government, the prerogatives of the executive branch in preparing its budgetary proposals, and the role of parliament in scrutinising and authorising the budget, are governed by convention rather than by an organic budget law. Nonetheless, there are a number of avenues open to the government to codify its gender budgeting practices.

In line with the OECD Review recommendations in this area, the Government of Canada announced in Budget 2018 that it will ask the Standing Committee on Procedure and House Affairs to examine making it a requirement that when any Minister of Finance tables a Budget in the House of Commons, a GBA+ analysis of the budget documents must be tabled concurrently. This would provide a sustainable and enduring basis for the practice into the future and bring the Canadian approach in line with OECD best practice.

Building a corpus of gender-disaggregated data

The GBA+ of the budget and wider gender budgeting efforts will only ever be as good as the data that informs them. FIN should to continue to highlight areas of policy where there is room for improvement in GBA+, as it did within the 2018 Equalities Chapter. This will help reinforce the efforts of SWC, TBS and departments in this area.

Improved GBA+ will require more in-depth gender-disaggregated data than are currently available. The Budget 2018 proposal to invest \$6.7 million over five years for Statistics Canada to create a new Centre for Gender, Diversity and Inclusion Statistics, a Centre that will act as GBA+ data hub will be particularly helpful in moving forward in this regard. Budget 2018 also proposes to provide \$5 million per year to Status of Women

Canada to undertake research and data collection in support of the Government's Gender Results Framework.

The Department of Finance as an advocate for gender budgeting

Government departments are usually in a better position to drive institutional change when they "practice what they preach". In particular, FIN has an opportunity to act as an advocate for gender budgeting by strengthening gender mainstreaming and the quality of GBA+ in its own policy areas, as is the case in Sweden (see Box 5.6). The announcement as part of Budget 2018 that FIN will extend the reach of GBA+ to examine tax expenditures was particularly welcome in this regard.

Box 5.6. Role of the Swedish Ministry of Finance in gender mainstreaming

Apart from responsibility for coordinating the budget work, the Ministry of Finance has five policy areas of its own. The Ministry has appointed four gender equality coordinators who work within the various areas of responsibility at the Ministry. Some examples of the Finance Ministry's gender mainstreaming work are outlined below.

Making gender visible in distributional analysis: The Finance Ministry's Economic Department is responsible for producing a special distribution policy appendix to the Spring Fiscal Policy Bill. Cognisant of its gender mainstreaming role, the Department introduced changes to make gender visible throughout the distributional policy appendix.

Improved gender guidance in budget circulars: The Ministry of Finance's Budget Department has worked with the Government Offices' Gender Equality Division in drawing up the directions sent to all ministries regarding the forthcoming Budget Bill. The ambition has been to make the gender perspective clearer in these steering documents.

Gender perspective on tax reforms: The Finance Ministry's Tax Department developed improved methods for analysing tax legislation proposals from a gender equality perspective

Applying a gender perspective to briefing material for international negotiations: The Finance Ministry's International Department has begun work with the objective of introducing gender equality aspects into briefing material for international negotiation work within bodies such as the EU, IMF and OECD. The point of departure here is economic efficiency from a gender equality perspective.

Source: (Government of Sweden, 2007[65])

To facilitate its role as the leader and advocate for gender budgeting, FIN may also benefit from increasing its gender economics capacity. In order to work effectively as partners, it is also recommended that SWC should increase its economics capacity. Indeed, SWC received significant new funding as part of Budget 2018 which can help it do this. This cross-fertilisation of skillsets will enable more gainful conversations between FIN and SWC.

This expert capacity would support the government in delivering its commitment to extend the reach of GBA+ to examine tax expenditures, federal transfers and the existing spending base, including the Estimates. It could also provide the scope for FIN, SWC and Statistics Canada to work together and research some of the more challenging topics in the area of gender budgeting, supporting the policy development work of departments and improved resource allocation decisions. Research might focus on topics such as the gender impact of policies in "hard-to-understand" areas (such as environment), or the assessment of the extent to which macroeconomic investment decisions (such as infrastructure versus social spending) can act as a hindrance or a catalyst for gender equality. The publication of such research would help develop the evidence base for departmental policy-making (see Section 2.2.5) and push the frontier for GBA+ and gender budgeting in Canada.

Measuring the impact of gender budgeting

Gender budgeting is a new tool for the Canadian Government and, as with any new tool, it is important to have a measurement framework in place that is capable of assessing the extent to which it is delivering the intended results. The Gender Results Framework provides a useful tool in terms of tracking broad progress in achieving gender equality objectives across different areas.

Given that – in addition to government policy - there are many factors which can impact progress towards gender equality objectives, it would also be useful for FIN to develop an additional evaluation mechanism which is able to capture how policies and resource allocation decisions change as a result of gender budgeting. Such information may be difficult to obtain for a number of reasons. For example, it may be difficult to identify the influence of gender budgeting on policy as it will not show up as a discrete step in the policy development process and it will be difficult to control for the impacts of political leadership and direction. However, any information that can be presented on the impact of gender budgeting will help stakeholders better understand its merits and support cultural change within public policy making. Ongoing evaluation could be conducted by FIN or another government agency (as is the case in Sweden, see Box 5.7).

Box 5.7. Measuring the impact of gender budgeting in Sweden

The Swedish Government have given the Swedish National Financial Management Authority (ESV), a government agency, responsibility for measuring the impact of gender budgeting reforms that have been carried out by the government. The agency will look at the impact of gender budgeting reforms as well as other budget reforms that may have had an impact on gender equality. It is hoped that the assessments will provide improved awareness of the wide range of budgeting factors which can contribute to or reduce gender equality. This will put the Swedish Government in a better position to put measures in place that correct these inequalities.

Source: Government of Sweden 2017

The government could also engage local or international experts to periodically review gender budgeting efforts. Case studies may also provide useful insights into how gender budgeting is influencing policy development, overall resource allocation and gender outcomes, as well as the barriers it is facing, can help improve its effectiveness over time.

Ensuring gender budgeting is open to critical perspectives

In keeping with its role in promoting a profound consideration and re-appraisal of budgeting choices and priorities, it is important that gender budgeting should not lose contact with its feminist-inspired origins and critical perspectives. Allowing gender budgeting to be introduced on a superficial basis, with facile modifications of existing processes and procedures, would not allow for the necessary "challenge" function to be introduced within policy-making; and would undermine wider trust in the ability of gender budgeting to bring about radical change to pre-existing policies and to the disposition of public resources. As one strategy to ensure that gender budgeting retains its critical focus, it is advisable that civil society be engaged in a meaningful way with the design and implementation of national approaches[3].

The consultative approach that has been initiated by FIN, in the context of developing the 2017 Gender Statement and 2018 Equalities Chapter, through the incorporation of a gender perspective to pre-budget consultations, should be built upon, developed and refined so that the views of civil society stakeholders on gender issues are taken into account in a more systematic and timely manner. In line with findings in Section 4.2.2, specific recommendations arising from OECD and other international good practice[4] are to:

- Establish a fixed calendar for timely consultation at key stages of the budget cycle (*ex ante* and *ex post*);
- Make explicit the purposes, scope and process of civil society engagement;
- Publically reporting on the extent to which the findings of the consultation process have been reflected in the budget; and
- Provide information about budgetary constraints and policy costings, as well as maximum transparency regarding the findings of GBA+ reports, so as to promote realistic and informed discussion of priorities and trade-offs.

Given that Canada is a large country, it may also be useful to cover travel expenses and/or allow videoconferencing to ensure the participation of citizen's groups which may have limited financial and human resources.

5.2.5. Subnational gender budgeting developments

The independence of the subnational governments in the conduct of their internal affairs is a fundamental constitutional principle in Canada (see section 2.4). As a result, the gender budgeting developments at the federal level have no direct implications for the other levels of government in terms of how they prepare their budgets. However, a number of provincial and municipal governments, such as Alberta, New Brunswick, and Ontario along with Edmonton and Toronto are considering how to take forward their own gender budgeting initiatives (see Box 5.8).

Box 5.8. Examples of gender budgeting at the subnational level in Canada

Alberta

When the Government of Alberta created the province's first Ministry of Status of Women in 2015, it made a commitment to advancing gender equality. Its approach is based on four pillars: gender budgeting, GBA+, data and analytics, engagement and community capacity building.

The Government of Alberta is introducing gender budgeting through a phased approach. For Budget 2018, a gender budgeting statement identifies spending on programmes and initiatives that have a positive impact on gender equality, and areas which require additional work. Alberta's commitment to these priorities was identified in ministry business plans and the government's strategic plan.

At full implementation, the Government of Alberta is looking to use gender budgeting as a tool to incorporate gender and diversity perspectives into the design, development, adoption, and execution of all business cycle processes, including Business Plans and Annual Reports so that financial planners can allocate resources where they are most needed and where they will have the greatest overall impact for gender equality.

Source: Government of Alberta 2018

Edmonton

Beginning in 2017, Edmonton City Administration committed to implementing broad based GBA+ training to share responsibility among the City's senior leadership for providing guidance, resources and support to enable the broad adoption of GBA+ throughout the organisation. To date more than 400 City staff, including 80 percent of senior leaders, have completed GBA+ training.

The City Administration also intends to begin testing the use of GBA+ analysis as a corporate business planning tool in alignment with the 2019-2022 budget cycle. During 2019-2022 business planning, City Administration will complete a GBA+ analysis for select City policies, services and/or initiatives to understand how they impact and are experienced by diverse Edmontonians. These analyses will provide an additional lens to understand the potential GBA+ implications of the selected City policies, services and initiatives at the planning stage, and may be used by City business areas to shape budget requests to enable a more equitable approach to select policies, services and initiatives.

The City will also prepare a summary that identifies spending on programs and initiatives that have a positive impact on gender equality, along with areas where a GBA+ lens can be used to plan for more equitable outcomes for diverse Edmontonians. Together, all of this testing will support City Administration in exploring how to apply a GBA+ lens more broadly as part of corporate business planning in the future.

Source: City of Edmonton 2018

While the autonomy of subnational governments helps to foster a range of innovative approaches to gender budgeting, there are practical implications in terms of ensuring that good practices are disseminated. More importantly, many issues of gender equality have commonalities, and indeed dependencies, that transcend the various levels of government in Canada. One notable example is the intersectionality between gender and the experiences of Indigenous peoples throughout Canada. Addressing such issues in an optimal way would benefit from some degree of practical coordination and knowledge-sharing among the various authorities, while respecting the legal and constitutional prerogatives of the various entities in question.

While the modalities of such coordination are beyond the scope of this OECD review, it is notable that some preliminary work in this area is already in train among some of the authorities at the various levels of government. It may also be advisable for FIN and SWC to facilitate this more coordinated approach, through convening a cross-government working group on gender budgeting aimed at sharing best practice, and exchanging insights on how policy goals might best be coordinated and sequenced among the national

Notes

[1] Other OECD countries to have introduced gender budgeting are: Austria, Belgium, Chile, Finland, Germany, Iceland, Ireland, Israel, Italy, Japan, Korea, Mexico, Portugal, Spain and Sweden (OECD, Forthcoming[58]).

[2] For more information, see - http://www.oecd-ilibrary.org/fr/taxation/the-impact-of-tax-and-benefit-systems-on-the-workforce-participation-incentives-of-women_d950acfc-en;jsessionid=73v93jehhcuhc.x-oecd-live-02

[3] A. O'Hagan, E. Klatzer (eds.) (2018), *Gender Budgeting in Europe*, - https://doi.org/10.1007/978-3-319-64891-0_1

[4] See OECD (2017) Budget Transparency Toolkit; OECD (2016).

References

Andalusian Regional Government Administration (2014), *PROGRESS IN THE ANDALUSIAN GRB INITIATIVE: GENDER AUDITS*, https://www.wu.ac.at/fileadmin/wu/d/i/vw3/Session_3_Cirujano_Gualda_Romero.pdf (accessed on 17 May 2018). [54]

Australian Government((n.d.)), *National Women's Alliances | Department of the Prime Minister and Cabinet*, 2018, https://www.pmc.gov.au/office-women/grants-and-funding/national-womens-alliances (accessed on 17 May 2018). [48]

Batliwala, S., S. Rosenhek and J. Miller (2013), "WOMEN MOVING MOUNTAINS: COLLECTIVE IMPACT OF THE DUTCH MDG3 FUND HOW RESOURCES ADVANCE WOMEN'S RIGHTS AND GENDER EQUALITY", https://www.awid.org/sites/default/files/atoms/files/Women%20Moving%20Mountains.pdf. [46]

Bochel, H. and A. Berthier (2018), *SPICe Briefing: Committee witnesses: gender and representation*, https://sp-bpr-en-prod-cdnep.azureedge.net/published/2018/2/27/Committee-witnesses--gender-and-representation/SB%2018-16.pdf (accessed on 17 May 2018). [52]

Bohnet, I. (2016), *What works: Gender Equality by Design*, Harvard University Press. [16]

Canadian Feminist Alliance for International Action (FAFIA) (2016), *Because its 2016! A National Gender Equality Plan*, http://tbinternet.ohchr.org/Treaties/CEDAW/Shared%20Documents/CAN/INT_CEDAW_NGO_CAN_25417_E.pdf (accessed on 12 December 2017). [23]

Canadian Institute for Advanced Research & Vancouver School of Economics (2016), *Earnings Inequality and the Gender Pay Gap*, http://faculty.arts.ubc.ca/nfortin/Fortin_EarningsInequalityGenderPayGap.pdf. [6]

Catalyst (2017), *Women In Male-Dominated Industries And Occupations*, http://www.catalyst.org/knowledge/women-male-dominated-industries-and-occupations. [10]

Congressional Budget Office (2016), *CBO's 2016 Long-Term Projections for Social Security: Additional Information*, https://www.cbo.gov/sites/default/files/114th-congress-2015-2016/reports/52298-socialsecuritychartbook.pdf. [62]

Downes, R., L. Von Trapp and S. Nicol (2016), "Gender budgeting in OECD countries", *OECD Journal on Budgeting* 3, http://www.oecd.org/gender/Gender-Budgeting-in-OECD-countries.pdf. [59]

EIGE (2018), *Spain – Structures*, http://eige.europa.eu/gender-mainstreaming/countries/spain/structures. [27]

European Parliament (2016), *Report on Gender Mainstreaming in the work of the European Parliament - A8-0034/2016*, http://www.europarl.europa.eu/sides/getDoc.do?type=REPORT&reference=A8-2016-0034&language=EN (accessed on 17 May 2018). [51]

European Parliament (2003), *European Parliament resolution on gender mainstreaming in the European Parliament (2002/2025(INI))*, http://www.europarl.europa.eu/sides/getDoc.do?pubRef=-//EP//TEXT+TA+P5-TA-2003-0098+0+DOC+XML+V0//EN. [50]

Flumian, M. (2016), "What Trudeau's committees tell us about his government | Institute on Governance", *Institute on Governance*, https://iog.ca/research-publications/publications/what-trudeaus-committees-tell-us-about-his-government/ (accessed on 21 January 2018). [29]

Goldin, C. (2014), "A Grand Gender Convergence: Its Last Chapter", *American Economic Review*, Vol. 104/4, pp. 1091-1119. [5]

Government of Canada (2018), *Budget 2018: Equality + Growth, A Strong Middle Class*, https://www.budget.gc.ca/2018/docs/plan/budget-2018-en.pdf. [8]

Government of Canada (2018), *Budget Plan + Growth*, https://financebudget.azurewebsites.net/2018/docs/plan/chap-01-en.html?wbdisable=true. [7]

Government of Canada (2018), *Innovation, Science and Economic Development Canada - Canada.ca*, https://www.canada.ca/en/innovation-science-economic-development.html. [44]

Government of Canada (2018), *Mandate Letter Tracker: Delivering results for Canadians*, https://www.canada.ca/en/privy-council/campaigns/mandate-tracker-results-canadians.html (accessed on 10 February 2018). [33]

Government of Canada (2018), *Policy on Results*, https://www.tbs-sct.gc.ca/pol/doc-eng.aspx?id=31300 (accessed on 17 May 2018). [38]

Government of Canada (2017), *Budget 2017: Building a Strong Middle Class*, https://www.budget.gc.ca/2017/docs/plan/budget-2017-en.pdf. [57]

Government of Canada (2017), *Fact Sheet: It's time to pay attention*, http://www.swc-cfc.gc.ca/violence/strategy-strategie/fs-fi-3-en.html. [45]

Government of Canada (2017), *Multilateral Early Learning and Child Care Framework - Canada.ca*, https://www.canada.ca/en/employment-social-development/programs/early-learning-child-care/reports/2017-multilateral-framework.html (accessed on 11 December 2017). [24]

Government of Canada (2017), *Results and Delivery in Canada: Building on momentum*, http://www.fmi.ca/media/1200856/results_and_delivery_building_momentum_october_2017.pdf. [34]

Government of Canada (2016), *Fall Economic Statement 2016*, https://www.budget.gc.ca/fes-eea/2016/docs/statement-enonce/fes-eea-2016-eng.pdf. [56]

Government of Canada (2016), *Increasing Recruitment of Women into the Canadian Armed Forces*. [17]

Government of Canada((n.d.)), *Charter Statements - Canada's System of Justice*, 2018, http://www.justice.gc.ca/eng/csj-sjc/pl/charter-charte/index.html (accessed on 17 May 2018). [41]

Government of Canada((n.d.)), *Employment Insurance Service Quality Review Report: Making Citizens Central*, 2017, https://www.canada.ca/en/employment-social-development/programs/ei/ei-list/reports/service-quality-review-report.html. [43]

Government of Finland (2016), *Government Action Plan For Gender Equality 2016–2019*, https://julkaisut.valtioneuvosto.fi/bitstream/handle/10024/79305/03_2017_Tasa-arvo-ohjelma_Enkku_kansilla.pdf?sequence=1. [19]

Government of Iceland((n.d.)), *Gender Budgeting*, 2018, https://www.government.is/topics/economic-affairs-and-public-finances/gender-budgeting/ (accessed on 16 May 2018). [60]

Government of Spain (2014), *Plan Estratégico de Igualdad de Oportunidades 2014-2016*, http://www.inmujer.gob.es/actualidad/PEIO/docs/PEIO2014-2016.pdf. [20]

Government of Sweden (2014), *Sweden's follow-up of the Platform for Action from the UN's*, https://www.regeringen.se/contentassets/b2f5cc340526433f8e33df3024d510e3/swedens-follow-up-of-the-platform-for-action-from-the-uns-fourth-world-conference-on-women-in-beijing-1995---covering-the-period-between-20092014. [47]

Government of Sweden (2007), *Moving Ahead: Gender budgeting in Sweden*, http://store1.digitalcity.eu.com/store/clients/release/AAAAGNJH/doc/gender-budgeting-in-sweden_2007.09.29-12.22.48.pdf. [65]

House of Commons Canada (2008), *Committee Report No. 9 - FEWO (39-2) - House of Commons of Canada*, http://www.ourcommons.ca/DocumentViewer/en/39-2/FEWO/report-9/. [53]

House of Commons Canada (2007), *Report of the Standing Committee on the Status of Women: The impacts of funding and program changes at Status of Women Canada*, http://www.ourcommons.ca/Content/Committee/391/FEWO/Reports/RP2876038/feworp18/feworp18-e.pdf (accessed on 23 January 2018). [26]

House of Commons Canada((n.d.)), *FEWO - About*, 2018, https://www.ourcommons.ca/Committees/en/FEWO/About (accessed on 17 May 2018). [49]

IMF (2017), *Gender Budgeting in G7 Countries*, https://www.imf.org/en/Publications/Policy-Papers/Issues/2017/05/12/pp041917gender-budgeting-in-g7-countries. [36]

Mahony, T. (2011), "Women and the Criminal Justice System", *Statistics Canada Catalogue no. 89-503-X*, http://www.statcan.gc.ca/pub/89-503-x/2010001/article/11416-eng.pdf (accessed on 17 May 2018). [11]

McInturff, K. and B. Lambert (2016), *Making Women Count: The Unequal Economics of Women's Work*, | Canadian Centre for Policy Alternatives, OXFAM Canada, https://www.policyalternatives.ca/publications/reports/making-women-count-0 (accessed on 01 January 2018). [13]

McKinsey Global Institute (2017), *The power of parity: Advancing women's equality in Canada*, https://www.mckinsey.com/featured-insights/gender-equality/the-power-of-parity-advancing-womens-equality-in-canada (accessed on 16 May 2018). [2]

Moyser, M. (2017), *Women and Paid Work, Statistics Canada, March, available online at: http://www.statcan.gc.ca/pub/89-503-x/2015001/article/14694-eng.htm.* [4]

OECD (2017), *Behavioural Insights and Public Policy: Lessons from Around the World.*, OECD Publishing. [15]

OECD (2017), *Building an inclusive Mexico : Policies and Good Governance for Gender Equality*, OECD Publishing. [28]

OECD (2017), *Recommendation of the Council on Open Government*, http://www.oecd.org/gov/Recommendation-Open-Government-Approved-Council-141217.pdf. [42]

OECD (2017), *The Pursuit of Gender Equality: An Uphill Battle*, OECD Publishing, Paris, http://dx.doi.org/10.1787/9789264281318-en. [1]

OECD (2016), *Open Government The Global Context and the Way Forward*, OECD Publishing. [32]

OECD (2016), "Open Government: The Global Context and The Way Forward", http://www.oecd-ilibrary.org/docserver/download/4216481e.pdf?expires=1516890637&id=id&accname=ocid84004878&checksum=36020513E75CAF56257B41F9DC2A3AFC (accessed on 25 January 2018). [31]

OECD (2015), "Delivering from the Centre: Strengthening the role of the centre of government in driving priority strategies", https://www.oecd.org/gov/cog-2015-delivering-priority-strategies.pdf (accessed on 21 January 2018). [25]

OECD (Forthcoming), *Budgeting in Austria.* [37]

OECD (Forthcoming), *Budgeting Outlook 2018.* [39]

OECD (Forthcoming), *Budgeting Practices and Procedures Dataset.* [58]

OECD (Forthcoming), *Governance Guidelines for Gender Budgeting.* [64]

OECD (forthcoming) (2018), *OECD Economic Surveys: Canada, OECD Publishing, Paris.* [3]

Office of the Auditor General Canada (2016), *Implementing Gender-Based Analysis*, http://www.oag-bvg.gc.ca/internet/English/parl_oag_201602_01_e_41058.html (accessed on 24 January 2018). [30]

Office of the Auditor General of Canada((n.d.)), *The Environment and Sustainable Development Guide*, 2018, http://www.oag-bvg.gc.ca/internet/English/meth_lp_e_19275.html (accessed on 17 May 2018). [55]

OXFAM Canada (2017), *Feminist Scorecard 2017: Tracking government action to advance women's rights and gender equality*, http://www.oxfam.ca (accessed on 11 December 2017). [22]

Schratzenstaller, M. (2014), *The implementation of gender responsive budgeting in Austria as central element of a major budget reform*, https://www.wu.ac.at/fileadmin/wu/d/i/vw3/Session_4_Schratzenstaller.pdf. [35]

Sharp, R. and R. Broomhill (2013), *A Case Study of Gender Responsive Budgeting in Australia*, https://consultations.worldbank.org/Data/hub/files/grb_papers_australia_updf_final.pdf. [63]

Status of Women Canada (2017), *It's Time: Canada's Strategy To Prevent and Address Gender-based Violence*, Government of Canada, http://www.swc-cfc.gc.ca/violence/strategy-strategie/GBV_Fact_sheets_2.pdf (accessed on 01 January 2018). [12]

Status of Women Canada((n.d.)), *The History of GBA+ Domestic and International Milestones.* [14]

Swedish Fiscal Policy Council (2016), *Finanspolitiska rådets rapport 2016*, http://www.finanspolitiskaradet.com/download/18.21a8337f154abc1a5dd28c15/1463487699296/Svensk+finanspolitik+2016.pdf. [61]

The Victorian Government (2018), *Safe and Strong: A Victorian Gender Equality Strategy. Achievements Report Year One*, https://www.vic.gov.au/system/user_files/Documents/women/1801009_Safe_and_strong_first_year_report_summary_10_%C6%92_web.pdf (accessed on 17 May 2018). [18]

UK National Audit Office (2016), *Sustainability in the spending review*, https://www.nao.org.uk/wp-content/uploads/2016/07/Sustainability-in-the-Spending-Review.pdf. [40]

United Nations (2016), "Concluding observations on the combined eighth and ninth periodic reports of Canada*", https://documents-dds-ny.un.org/doc/UNDOC/GEN/N16/402/03/PDF/N1640203.pdf?OpenElement (accessed on 11 December 2017). [21]

Wells, M. (2018), *Closing the Engineering Gender Gap*, https://www.design-engineering.com/features/engineering-gender-gap/. [9]

ORGANISATION FOR ECONOMIC CO-OPERATION AND DEVELOPMENT

The OECD is a unique forum where governments work together to address the economic, social and environmental challenges of globalisation. The OECD is also at the forefront of efforts to understand and to help governments respond to new developments and concerns, such as corporate governance, the information economy and the challenges of an ageing population. The Organisation provides a setting where governments can compare policy experiences, seek answers to common problems, identify good practice and work to co-ordinate domestic and international policies.

The OECD member countries are: Australia, Austria, Belgium, Canada, Chile, the Czech Republic, Denmark, Estonia, Finland, France, Germany, Greece, Hungary, Iceland, Ireland, Israel, Italy, Japan, Korea, Latvia, Luxembourg, Mexico, the Netherlands, New Zealand, Norway, Poland, Portugal, the Slovak Republic, Slovenia, Spain, Sweden, Switzerland, Turkey, the United Kingdom and the United States. The European Union takes part in the work of the OECD.

OECD Publishing disseminates widely the results of the Organisation's statistics gathering and research on economic, social and environmental issues, as well as the conventions, guidelines and standards agreed by its members.

OECD PUBLISHING, 2, rue André-Pascal, 75775 PARIS CEDEX 16
(42 2018 28 1 P) ISBN 978-92-64-30109-2 – 2018

www.ingramcontent.com/pod-product-compliance
Ingram Content Group UK Ltd.
Pitfield, Milton Keynes, MK11 3LW, UK
UKHW051506290926
15471UKWH00008B/1442

9 789264 301092